Revolutions: A Very Short Introduction

VERY SHORT INTRODUCTIONS are for anyone wanting a stimulating and accessible way into a new subject. They are written by experts, and have been translated into more than 45 different languages.

The series began in 1995, and now covers a wide variety of topics in every discipline. The VSI library currently contains over 700 volumes—a Very Short Introduction to everything from Psychology and Philosophy of Science to American History and Relativity—and continues to grow in every subject area.

Very Short Introductions available now:

ABOLITIONISM Richard S. Newman
THE ABRAHAMIC RELIGIONS
  Charles L. Cohen
ACCOUNTING Christopher Nobes
ADDICTION Keith Humphreys
ADOLESCENCE Peter K. Smith
THEODOR W. ADORNO
  Andrew Bowie
ADVERTISING Winston Fletcher
AERIAL WARFARE Frank Ledwidge
AESTHETICS Bence Nanay
AFRICAN AMERICAN HISTORY
  Jonathan Scott Holloway
AFRICAN AMERICAN RELIGION
  Eddie S. Glaude Jr
AFRICAN HISTORY John Parker and
  Richard Rathbone
AFRICAN POLITICS Ian Taylor
AFRICAN RELIGIONS
  Jacob K. Olupona
AGEING Nancy A. Pachana
AGNOSTICISM Robin Le Poidevin
AGRICULTURE Paul Brassley and
  Richard Soffe
ALEXANDER THE GREAT
  Hugh Bowden
ALGEBRA Peter M. Higgins
AMERICAN BUSINESS HISTORY
  Walter A. Friedman
AMERICAN CULTURAL HISTORY
  Eric Avila
AMERICAN FOREIGN RELATIONS
  Andrew Preston
AMERICAN HISTORY
  Paul S. Boyer

AMERICAN IMMIGRATION
  David A. Gerber
AMERICAN INTELLECTUAL
  HISTORY Jennifer
  Ratner-Rosenhagen
THE AMERICAN JUDICIAL
  SYSTEM Charles L. Zelden
AMERICAN LEGAL HISTORY
  G. Edward White
AMERICAN MILITARY HISTORY
  Joseph T. Glatthaar
AMERICAN NAVAL HISTORY
  Craig L. Symonds
AMERICAN POETRY David Caplan
AMERICAN POLITICAL HISTORY
  Donald Critchlow
AMERICAN POLITICAL PARTIES
  AND ELECTIONS L. Sandy Maisel
AMERICAN POLITICS
  Richard M. Valelly
THE AMERICAN PRESIDENCY
  Charles O. Jones
THE AMERICAN REVOLUTION
  Robert J. Allison
AMERICAN SLAVERY
  Heather Andrea Williams
THE AMERICAN SOUTH
  Charles Reagan Wilson
THE AMERICAN WEST Stephen Aron
AMERICAN WOMEN'S HISTORY
  Susan Ware
AMPHIBIANS T. S. Kemp
ANAESTHESIA Aidan O'Donnell
ANALYTIC PHILOSOPHY
  Michael Beaney

Available soon:

For more information visit our website

www.oup.com/vsi/

Jack A. Goldstone

REVOLUTIONS

A Very Short Introduction

SECOND EDITION

OXFORD
UNIVERSITY PRESS

Oxford University Press is a department of the University of Oxford.
It furthers the University's objective of excellence in research, scholarship,
and education by publishing worldwide. Oxford is a registered trade mark of
Oxford University Press in the UK and in certain other countries.

Published in the United States of America by Oxford University Press
198 Madison Avenue, New York, NY 10016, United States of America.

Library of Congress Cataloging-in-Publication Data

Names: Goldstone, Jack A., author.
Title: Revolutions : a very short introduction / Jack A. Goldstone.
Description: Second edition. | New York, NY : Oxford University Press,
[2023] | "First Edition published in 2014" — Title page verso.
Identifiers: LCCN 2023034385 (print) | LCCN 2023034386 (ebook) |
ISBN 9780197666302 (paperback) | ISBN 9780197666326 (epub)
Subjects: LCSH: Revolutions—History.
Classification: LCC D21.3 .G65 2023 (print) | LCC D21.3 (ebook) |
DDC 303.6/409—dc23/eng/20230722
LC record available at https://lccn.loc.gov/2023034385
LC ebook record available at https://lccn.loc.gov/2023034386

Printed and bound by CPI Group (UK) Ltd, Croydon, CR0 4YY

To my wife, Gina, who makes everything possible

Contents

Revolutions

List of illustrations

Acknowledgments

I am grateful to fellow scholars of revolution for their comments on parts of the manuscript:

Mark Beissinger, Steven Cook, William Doyle, John Foran, Stephen Haber, Richard Hamilton, Mark Kishlansky, Alan Knight, Charles Kurzman, John Markoff, John May, Ian Morris, Sharon Erickson Nepstad, John Padgett, Silvia Pedraza, Elizabeth Perry, Eric Selbin, S. A. Smith, Walter Scheidel, and Gordon Wood. They have saved me from many errors; I bear responsibility for those that remain.

I also owe major debts to my editors at Oxford University Press—Nancy Toff, Joellyn Ausanka, Chelsea Hogue, and Max Richman—for their encouragement, support, exacting review, and superb execution of this volume. Their insistence on quality in every respect is a model for editors.

My wonderful wife, Gina Saleman-Goldstone, reviewed each chapter for clarity and style; if this book is easy and enjoyable to read, the credit goes to her.

Chapter 1
What is a revolution?

On the morning of July 14, 1789, a crowd of Parisian workers set out to attack the royal prison of the Bastille. Joined by deserting soldiers who brought cannons, and ignored by Royal Army troops camped nearby, the crowds forced their way into the fortress by late afternoon, killing the governor and parading his head on a pike. That evening King Louis XVI reportedly asked the Duc de la Rochefoucauld, "Is this a revolt?" To which the duc replied: "No, sire, it is a *revolution!*"

The duc's answer was shaped by his awareness that the crowds of Paris were not simply demanding lower prices for bread, or the dismissal of an unpopular minister, or protesting the selfish luxury of the queen, Marie Antoinette. They were acting in support of the National Assembly, led by the representatives of the Third Estate, or commoners, to the Estates General. Three weeks earlier, the assembly had defied the king and declared that they, not the Estates of the Nobles or the Clergy, were the true leaders of France. If they were supported by the people and the military defected to join them, the old social and political order of France would be over.

Two great visions shape our views of revolution. One is the heroic vision of revolution. In this view, downtrodden masses are raised up by leaders who guide them in overthrowing unjust rulers, enabling the people to gain their freedom and dignity. Though revolutions are violent, this is necessary to destroy the old regime and vanquish its supporters—the birth pangs of a new order that will provide social justice. This ideal, rooted in Greek and Roman traditions of the founding of republics, was promoted by defenders of the American and French Revolutions such as Thomas Paine and Jules Michelet. It was later given modern form as a theory of the inevitable triumph of the poor over the rich by Karl Marx, Vladimir Lenin, Mao Zedong, and their followers.

Yet there is a second, opposing vision, that revolutions are eruptions of popular anger that produce chaos. In this view, however well-meaning, reformers who unleash the mob find the masses demanding blood and creating waves of violence that destroy even the revolutionary leaders. Chasing unrealistic visions and their own glory, revolutionary leaders lay waste to civilized society and bring unwarranted death and destruction. This view was promoted by English critics who feared the excesses of the French Revolution, from Edmund Burke and Thomas Carlyle to Charles Dickens. It was later taken up by critics of the Russian and Chinese revolutions who emphasized the human costs of the transformations pursued by Stalin and Mao.

In reality, the history of revolution reveals both faces. Actual revolutions are enormously varied. Some are nonviolent whereas others produce bloody civil wars; some have produced democracies and greater liberty whereas others have produced brutal dictatorships. Today, political leaders are less concerned with the contending myths of revolution than with understanding why revolutions occur and how they evolve. Revolutions erupting in unexpected places—in Iran and Nicaragua in 1979, in the Soviet Union and Eastern Europe in 1989–91, and across the Arab world in 2011—have not only come as shocks to rulers but have unsettled the international order.

This book seeks to answer the questions of why revolutions occur and why they surprise us, how they have developed over the course of history, and where they have shaped national and global politics. But first we need to have a clear idea of precisely what a revolution is, and how revolutions differ from other kinds of disorders and social change.

Defining "revolution"

Throughout history, people have suffered from misfortune and oppression. Most of the time, people respond with fortitude and resignation, or prayer and hope. Those who suffer usually see the forces in power as too great to change and view themselves as too isolated and weak to be agents of change. Even when people do rebel against authorities, most such acts remain isolated and are easily put down.

Revolutions are thus rare—much rarer than the instances of oppression and injustice. They arise only when rulers become weak and isolated, when elites begin to attack the government rather than defend it, and when people believe themselves to be part of a numerous, united, and righteous group that can act together to create change.

Scholars of politics and history have defined revolution in different ways. Most agree that revolutions involve a forcible change in government, mass participation, and a change in institutions. But some have argued that revolutions must be relatively sudden; others that they entail violence; and still others that revolutions involve class-based struggles of the poor against the rich and thereby transform the social order. Yet in fact revolutions are diverse in these respects.

In the Chinese Communist Revolution, Mao Zedong spent more than twenty years in the countryside mobilizing the peasantry and fighting the Nationalist regime before taking power. Most of the recent "color" revolutions, such as the People Power Revolution in the Philippines and the Orange Revolution in Ukraine, were rapid, unfolding in weeks; yet they remained nonviolent. And many anticolonial revolutions—such as the American Revolution—pitted members of all classes against the colonial power and produced little or no redistribution of wealth or social status.

For much of the twentieth century, social scientists were reluctant to deal with the subjective side of revolution. These "structuralists" preferred to focus on the more easily observed features of conflict and institutional change. Yet in recent years, students of revolution have come to realize how critical the ideologies and narratives of social justice are to revolutionary mobilization and revolutionary outcomes. The pursuit of social justice is inseparable from how people define their revolutionary identities and frame their actions.

We can therefore best define revolution in terms of *both* observed mass mobilization and institutional change, *and* a driving ideology carrying a vision of social justice. *Revolution* is the forcible overthrow of a government through mass mobilization (whether military or civilian or both) in the name of social justice, to create new political institutions.

What revolutions are not

A key difficulty in defining revolutions is separating them from similar, more common disruptive events, particularly since such events almost always occur as part of revolutions. These component events include peasant revolts, grain riots, strikes, social and reform movements, coup d'états, secessions, and civil wars. All of these have their own causes and outcomes, but only under certain conditions do they lead to revolutions.

Peasant revolts are uprisings of rural villages. They sometimes aim at resisting the demands of local landlords, sometimes at foiling state agents (tax collectors or other officials). Usually they seek to call attention to exceptional local hardships. Most often, their goal is to get help from the government to resolve local problems, not to change the government itself.

Grain riots are mass mobilizations to protest food shortages or excessively high prices. They involve seizures of grain shipments or stores, attacks on bakeries or merchants, and—in the style of Robin Hood—efforts to distribute food to the poor, and demands to enforce a maximum price or secure state subsidies. They usually occur in cities, where people depend on buying grain and other necessities at market prices, but they can also occur in rural areas at key points for the transit or storage of grain. Grain riots arose in more than a dozen African countries in the wake of high global food prices in 2007–8. Like peasant revolts, they usually seek government help, rather than to change the government.

Strikes are mobilizations of workers to withhold work from employers. They usually focus on workplace issues of pay, hours, safety, and work rules, and are local to a particular region or industry. However, if workers have widely shared grievances against the government they may seek a general strike, in which workers throughout the country refuse to work, or a political strike, in which workers in key industries (mining, energy, transport) coordinate a refusal to work until the government policies in question are changed. Such strikes were crucial in bringing down the Soviet and other communist regimes in Eastern Europe.

Peasant revolts and grain riots are typical of traditional agricultural societies. In most modern societies, by contrast, protests against government policies take the form of social or reform movements. Social movements are mass mobilizations on behalf of particular groups or causes. Social movements can be disruptive and provoke regime violence, as with the civil rights and anti-Vietnam war movements in the United States. They employ such tactics as sit-ins, marches, boycotts, and occupations of state buildings or public places. Nonetheless, most social movements simply aim for policy changes, not regime change.

Reform movements explicitly seek to change existing government institutions. They may seek new laws to limit corruption, or voting rights for more people, or greater autonomy for a region. Yet rather than seeking to overthrow the existing government, they try to attain their goals by working through lawful procedures for institutional change, seeking to win court rulings or electoral campaigns, pass new laws, or obtain constitutional changes. They become revolutionary only when the government resists or delays meaningful change and lashes out at reformers. Thus the Mexican Revolution was unleashed when the dictator Porfirio Díaz jailed the moderate reformer Francisco Madero and manipulated the results of elections that reformers appeared to have won.

While peasant revolts, strikes, and social and reform movements usually aim to remedy local or group grievances, other kinds of events do aim to overthrow the government. These include coups, secessions, and civil wars. But these do not usually produce revolutions either.

The most common acts that forcibly overthrow governments are coups d'état (literally, blows to the state). They occur when one authoritarian leader or a small group of leaders (most often from the military) takes over the government, without any large mass mobilization or civil struggle. Although coups against democracies or monarchies produce new political institutions, they hardly ever do so in the name of broad principles of social justice. Rather, the coup leaders usually claim their actions were necessary to restore order, end intolerable corruption, or halt economic decay, and that they will step down once their task is done. Recent military coups in Thailand in 2006 and in Niger in 2010 are good examples.

On the other hand, coups can lead to revolutions if the coup leaders or their followers present a vision for reshaping society on new principles of justice and social order, embark on a program of mass mobilization to build support for that vision, and then enact that vision by creating new institutions. Atäturk's secular nationalist revolution in Turkey, Nasser's Arab nationalist revolution in Egypt, and the Portuguese Officers' Revolution are all cases in point.

Secessions and civil wars often produce the forcible overthrow of governments (in the case of secession, the opposition seeks the overthrow of government authority in a particular region that wants to become independent). These events can arise from dynastic contests that pit claimants from the same family tree against each other; from military officers falling out and competing for power using their armed supporters; or from religious or ethnic groups seeking to oust or expel their rivals. But in none of these cases is the effort to overthrow the government driven by the dream of realizing a new vision of social justice. Only when leaders with a revolutionary vision seek to realize that vision via secession or overturning the central authority would we call such events a revolution.

Revolutionary civil wars also arise after the old regime has been overthrown. Those who enjoyed privileges under the old regime, or even those simply resisting unwelcome changes, may mobilize counterrevolutionary forces and go to war against the new revolutionary government. Some of the most massive civil wars in history, such as the Russian Whites against the Red Army in 1918–21, and the Mexican Civil War of 1913–20, both of which killed millions, arose when revolutionary leaders struggled against counterrevolutions.

In addition to the aforementioned events, one often hears the terms "rebellions, uprisings, insurrections, and guerrilla wars" used when talking about revolutions. These are general terms that are sometimes conflated with "revolution" but do not mean the same thing. A rebellion is any act by a group or individual that refuses to recognize, or seeks to overturn, the authority of the existing government. Thus one can have an elite rebellion, as when courts refuse to recognize a decree of the ruler; or one can have a popular rebellion, as when crowds occupy a public square and refuse to obey government demands that they disperse.

Any attempt at revolution is by definition a rebellion, so efforts to overthrow a regime that fail are often called rebellions. Still, not every rebellion that succeeds leads to revolution. If a duke with dynastic claims to the throne takes up arms against the king, that is a rebellion. But if the duke succeeds and becomes the new king, and all the institutions of government remain much the same, then no revolution has occurred. Uprisings and insurrections are types of popular rebellions—uprisings are usually unarmed or primitively armed popular rebellions, while insurrections involve some degree of military training and organization, and the use of military weapons and tactics by the rebels.

Guerrilla warfare is simply a style of warfare often used in rebellions and revolutions. Whereas conventional warfare relies on fighters who are massed in large-scale military units in regular formations, and who are housed in barracks and supplied by military supply trains, guerrilla warfare relies on smaller numbers of mobile fighters, in irregular-sized units, living off the land or blending into and supplied by the local population. Guerrilla warfare is particularly useful for small forces trying to expel a larger, more powerful force from their territory by inflicting a steady stream of losses while avoiding pitched battles with the more powerful foe. It is therefore often chosen by revolutionaries who are initially few in number and facing a powerful government. The Chinese Communists, the Viet Cong, Castro's forces in Cuba, and the Nicaraguan Sandinistas all used guerrilla warfare. However, as the numbers of their supporters increased and they gained access to more resources (often from abroad), they shifted to more conventional warfare in the final struggle for power.

Peasant revolts, grain riots, strikes, social movements, coups, secessions, and civil wars thus all can arise in the course of revolutions and are important constituent elements of revolutionary struggles. Nevertheless, a revolution is something distinct from any of these alone. What gives revolutions their distinctive role in history and the popular imagination is that only revolutions combine *all* the elements of forcible overthrow of the government, mass mobilization, the pursuit of a vision of social justice, and the creation of new political institutions. It is this combination that leads us to conceive of revolutions as *the process by which visionary leaders draw on the power of the masses to seek to forcibly bring into existence a new political order.*

Chapter 2
What causes revolutions?

A common misperception about revolutions is that they are acts of frustration—they happen when people say "We're mad as hell and we won't take it anymore." Yet scholarly research has shown that this view is wrong.

Let us start by asking "won't take any more of *what?*" One possible answer is poverty: when people are so poor that their very survival is threatened, they rebel. This is not entirely wrong, for economic grievances often play a role in rebellions. Yet poverty is generally *not* associated with revolution. The worst poverty usually arises in the wake of crop failures and famines, yet the majority of famines—such as the great Irish potato famine of the 1840s—did not lead to revolutions.

In fact, revolutions occur more often in middle-income countries than in the very poorest nations. When the American Revolution occurred, the American colonists were far better off than European peasants. Even in Europe, the French Revolution of 1789 arose in a country whose peasants were generally better off than the peasants of Russia, where revolution did not occur until more than a hundred years later.

This is because poor peasants and workers cannot overthrow the government when faced with professional military forces determined to defend the regime. Revolutions can occur only when significant portions of the elites, and especially the military, defect or stand aside. Indeed, in most revolutions it is the elites who mobilize the population to help them overthrow the regime.

Some scholars, recognizing that sheer poverty may produce popular revolts but not revolutions, have argued that it is *relative* deprivation that drives revolution—when inequality or class differences grow unbearable, or when people's expectations for further progress are dashed, they rise up in protest. But extreme inequality can just as easily lead to resignation and despair as to revolution; deep inequality also leaves the poor without the resources to create an effective revolutionary force. Throughout most of human history, great inequality and severe poverty have been justified by religion and tradition as natural and inevitable, and have been tolerated, even accepted, as the normal order of things.

What turns poverty or inequality into a motivation for revolution? It is the belief that these conditions are not inevitable but arise from the faults of the regime. Only when elites and popular groups blame the regime for unjust conditions—whether arising from the regime's incompetence, corruption, or favoritism for certain groups at the expense of others—will people rise against it.

Another force often blamed for revolutions is modernization. Many observers have argued that as preindustrial societies start to modernize, people encounter free markets for goods and services, inequality rises, and traditional religious and customary patterns of authority lose their power. As traditional relationships break down, people demand new, more responsive political regimes and turn to force to create them.

With more study, however, it is clear that modernization is not a single package of changes that arrived everywhere in the same way. In some countries modernizing changes undermined regimes and gave rise to revolutions; but in other countries modernizing changes strengthened rulers and created more powerful authoritarian regimes (as in Saudi Arabia today or Germany under Bismarck). In still others, such as Canada, modernization brought a relatively smooth transition to democracy. In a few nations revolutions occurred just as modernization was beginning, as in Japan in 1868 and China in 1911. Yet in other nations revolutions occurred long after modernization had been largely accomplished, as in Eastern Europe in 1989–91. Clearly, modernization has no consistent relationship to the onset of revolutions.

Finally, some observers attribute revolutions to the spread of new ideologies. This view too has some truth, as ideological shifts play an important role in revolutionary mobilization. Yet this does not explain why people would be drawn to dangerous new political ideas. Rulers and elites usually enforce beliefs that justify their rule, while harshly punishing those who question their authority. So revolutionary ideologies often languish without followers. New ideologies produce revolutionary actions only when there has already been a shift in elite positions, which creates space and opportunities to mobilize people around new beliefs. New ideologies are a part of the story of revolutions. But their appearance is not sufficient to produce revolutionary change.

The reason that all these views of revolutionary causation are inadequate is that they treat society as a passive structure—like a concrete wall—that will crumble when sufficient force is applied. Given enough poverty, inequality, modernization, or ideological change, the social order will collapse and revolution will occur. Yet society is not a passive structure. Rather, societies consist of millions of active people and groups whose actions continually re-create and reinforce the social order.

Rulers provide defense and services in return for taxes; elites provide support for rulers in return for prestige and political and material rewards; and popular groups engage in economic activities, raise families, pray in churches, and receive protection in return for their economic activity and political obedience. The whole of society is continually being reconstituted by multiple overlapping relationships. These relationships allow societies to reproduce themselves over time while also being resilient, able to bounce back and reconstitute themselves after famines, wars, epidemics, local rebellions, religious heresies, and other crises. As long as elites remain united and loyal to the regime, and most popular groups remain reasonably content and focused on managing their own lives, regimes can be stable for centuries despite considerable strains and crises.

Revolutions as complex emergent processes

To understand what causes revolutions, it is also necessary to understand what keeps societies stable and resilient. In a stable society, popular groups engage in economic activities that generate sufficient income to support themselves and their families, and to pay the rents and taxes that support elites and the government. Elites—both those working for the government and those leading other organizations—act as the critical intermediaries between the state and the populace, organizing political, economic, religious, and educational activities, reinforcing existing beliefs and behavior, and recruiting and training new elite members. The rulers provide rewards, recognition, and support to the elites, who in turn support the rulers' authority. Rulers also aim to protect the populace from banditry, invasions, famines, and other threats so that people can pay their rents and taxes. Under these conditions, a society is stable and resilient. It is resistant to the spread of rebellion and revolutionary ideologies because loyal military, bureaucratic, and religious elites will suppress opposition, and because most social groups are invested in the status quo and would not take major risks to change it.

Such a society can be described as being in "stable equilibrium." This concept comes from physical science. Imagine a ball sitting at the bottom of a large depression; if a small force moves the ball in any direction, it simply falls back into the depression, returning to its former state. Thus, a stable equilibrium is one in which the response to a moderate disturbance is a return to the original condition. Similarly, in a society in stable equilibrium, the response to a peasant revolt or strike, a war or economic crisis, is for rulers and elites and even most popular groups to act to restore the existing social order.

Yet consider what happens if the ball is not sitting in a depression, but resting on top of a hill. In the absence of any force the ball remains in place, but a small force pushing the ball now leads it to roll off the hill and head in a new direction. This is an unstable equilibrium—a small disturbance leads to an ever larger departure from the prior condition. This is precisely what happens to a society in a revolution.

When we examine societies in the years leading up to a revolution, we find that social relationships have changed. The rulers have become weakened, erratic, or predatory so that many of the elites no longer feel rewarded or supported, and are not inclined to support the regime. Elites are no longer unified but instead have become divided into mutually suspicious and distrusting factions. Popular groups find that their efforts are not providing them with expected rewards or outcomes. There may be shortages of land or work, excessive rents or falling real wages, and growing banditry, so that ordinary people are unsettled and distressed. Many elites and popular groups view the rulers and other elites as unjust; they are drawn to heterodox beliefs or ideologies that make sense of their grievances and offer solutions through social change. Rulers may attempt reforms, aiming to win elite or popular support and to gain additional resources. But these are usually too little and too late, and merely create more uncertainty and fresh opposition.

Under such conditions, a moderate or even small disturbance—a war, an economic crisis, a local rebellion, or an act of exceptional defiance or repression—can trigger spreading popular uprisings and heightened confrontations among elite groups. If a significant portion of the elites and diverse popular groups form a coalition against the rulers and demand major changes, a revolution has begun. If the military then suffers defections, and is reluctant or unable to overcome the spreading resistance, the revolution will succeed. This is how revolutions arise—over time, a society shifts from a condition of stable equilibrium to unstable equilibrium. Then even a small disorder can set off an accelerating movement toward greater disorder and the overturning of the existing regime.

Revolutions do not arise simply from mounting discontent over poverty, inequality, or other changes. Rather, revolution is a complex process that emerges from the social order becoming frayed in many areas at once.

Unstable equilibrium and the paradox of revolution

Unfortunately, it is not always easy to determine whether a country is in unstable equilibrium, as despite underlying changes it may appear outwardly stable for a long time. Strikes, demonstrations, or revolts may be dismissed as insignificant as long as they are small and the military or police are willing and able to repress them. The degree to which other groups sympathize with protests, or that there is disaffection in the military and police, may not be visible until after it is too late. Elites may hide their growing discord and opposition until they seize an opportunity to act against the regime. Rulers may embark on reforms believing they will succeed, or undertake repressive acts believing they will end all opposition; it may not be clear until later that reforms have failed to win support or that repression has triggered greater resentment and opposition.

Revolutions are thus like earthquakes. Geologists can identify major fault zones, and we know that earthquakes are most likely to arise in those zones. But a series of small tremors may be a release of tensions, or it may signify growing pressures that will soon produce a major shift; one cannot generally tell in advance. An earthquake may occur on a well-known fault, or it may erupt from a new or previously hidden fault line. Knowing the general mechanisms behind earthquakes has not allowed us to predict them. Similarly, social scientists can identify societies that seem to have major faults and growing tensions—these may be evident from signs of social conflict or heightened difficulties of institutions or groups carrying out accustomed tasks or meeting their goals. Yet that does not mean that we can predict exactly when a particular state will experience the shock of revolution.

Scholars of revolutions generally agree upon five elements that they consider necessary and sufficient to create an unstable social equilibrium from which revolutions can arise. First is national economic or fiscal strains; such conditions disrupt the flow of rents and taxes to rulers and elites and undermine the income of the general population. Such strains commonly lead rulers to increase taxes or borrow heavily, often in ways that seem unjust; they also hinder the rulers' ability to reward their supporters and pay their officials and military forces.

Second is growing alienation and opposition among the elites. Elites are always competing for position. Rivalries among families, parties, or factions are commonplace. However, a ruler usually can take advantage of this competition to win support from elites, by playing off groups against each other and rewarding loyalty. Stable elites also manage to recruit and absorb talented newcomers. Alienation occurs when elite groups feel they are being systematically and unjustly excluded from favor. Older elites may feel they are being unfairly displaced by newcomers, or new aspiring elites may feel their way forward is being unfairly blocked. Elites may feel that a narrow group—a small circle of cronies or members of the rulers' ethnic or regional group—is unfairly getting a dominant share of political power or economic rewards. Under these conditions, elites can believe that their loyalty will not be rewarded, and that the existing regime will always work to their disadvantage. They may then seek reforms, or if those are blocked or considered ineffective, elites may seek to mobilize and even try to take advantage of popular discontent to put pressure on the regime for change. As their alienation grows, they may aim to overturn and replace the existing social order, turning against the regime they had previously supported.

Third, revolutionary mobilization builds on some form of increasingly widespread popular anger at injustice. This popular anger need not be the result of extreme poverty or inequality. Rather, what matters is that people feel they are losing their proper place in society for reasons that are not inevitable and not their fault. These may be peasants who worry that they are losing access to the land or being saddled with excessive rents or taxes or other burdens; workers who find themselves unable to find employment or who face rising prices for necessities and stagnant wages; students who cannot find the jobs they expect and desire; or mothers who feel they cannot provide for their children. When these groups feel their difficulties are the result of unjust actions by elites or rulers, they will take the risks of joining in revolts to call attention to their plight and demand change.

Popular groups may act through their own local organizations, such as peasant communes and village councils, workers' unions, neighborhoods, student or youth organizations, and guilds or professional groups. They may also be mobilized by elites, civil or military, who recruit and organize the populace to challenge the government.

Popular groups may engage in urban marches, demonstrations, and occupations of public spaces. In the nineteenth century, the call "to the barricades" was a call to erect barriers to keep state forces out of "liberated" neighborhoods; today an occupation is more likely to fill a central space with crowds, such as Tahrir Square in Cairo. Workers may also call for boycotts and general strikes. If the revolutionaries deem the government's forces too strong to challenge in the capital, they may instead organize guerrilla forces in remote mountainous or forested areas and seek to gradually build up their strength.

Rebellions that remain local and isolated are usually easily suppressed. But if rebellion spreads to many regions and includes peasants, workers, and students, and these groups link up with elites, their resistance can become too extensive for government forces to deal with all at once. The revolutionary forces can then thrive in certain areas, evading government forces in some regions and striking in others. At some point, military officers or enlisted men may refuse to kill their own people to keep the government in power; at that point the defection or collapse of the military ushers in the victory of the revolutionary forces.

Fourth, bridging various popular and elite grievances and demands, and linking and mobilizing diverse groups, requires an ideology that presents a persuasive shared narrative of resistance. This may take the form of a new religious movement: fundamentalist religious groups, from English Puritanism to Jihadist Islam, have often justified revolt against an immoral ruler. It may take the form of a secular narrative against injustice, stressing the rights and the innocent victims who have been abused. It may be a narrative of nationalist liberation. Whatever their form, effective narratives of resistance highlight the terrible injustices of the current regime and create a sense of shared identity and righteousness among the opposition.

Although the elites may stress abstractions, such as the evils of capitalism or the importance of natural rights, the most effective narratives of resistance also draw on local traditions and stories of heroes who fought for justice in times past. American and French revolutionaries harked back to revolutionary episodes in ancient Greece and Rome. The Cuban and Nicaraguan Revolutions evoked the memory of earlier Cuban and Nicaraguan independence fighters, José Martí and Augusto César Sandino. Interestingly, research has shown that revolutionary ideologies need not provide a precise future plan to unite and motivate their followers. Rather, what works best are vague or utopian promises of better times ahead combined with a detailed and emotionally powerful depiction of the intolerable injustice and inescapable evils of the current regime.

Finally, a revolution requires favorable international relations. Revolutionary success has often depended on foreign support for the opposition coming at crucial times, or on the withdrawal of foreign support for the ruler. Conversely, many revolutions have failed or been reversed because of foreign intervention to support counterrevolution.

When these five conditions coincide—economic or fiscal strain, alienation and opposition among the elites, widespread popular anger at injustice, a persuasive shared narrative of resistance, and favorable international relations—the normal social mechanisms that restore order in crises are unlikely to work. Instead, societies where these conditions prevail are in an unstable equilibrium, where any untoward event can trigger escalating popular revolts and open elite resistance, producing a revolution.

Yet for all five of these conditions to coincide is rare. Moreover, they are difficult to assess accurately during periods of apparent stability. States may obfuscate their finances until they suddenly face bankruptcy; elites typically hide their disloyalty until they see an opportunity to act; and popular groups may seethe with inward anger but give few hints of how far they will go. Narratives of resistance may circulate discreetly underground or in hidden cells; whether other states will intervene to support or oppose a revolution is often unknown until the revolutionary struggle has begun.

The difficulty in determining whether outward stability represents a stable or unstable equilibrium produces the paradox of revolutions: In hindsight, after a revolution has occurred, it is quite apparent how severely the finances of governments and elites were affected by economic or fiscal strain; how much elites were alienated and divided from the regime; how widely felt were pangs of anger and injustice; how persuasive were the revolutionary narratives; and that international conditions were favorable. Indeed, it becomes possible to explain the origins of a revolution in such detail that its onset seems, in retrospect, inevitable. Yet at the same time, when revolutions do occur, they usually come as a complete shock to everyone, including the rulers, the revolutionaries themselves, and foreign powers. Lenin famously remarked in January 1917, just weeks before the Russian regime collapsed, that "We of the older generation may not live to see the decisive battles of this coming revolution."

This is because no one is usually positioned to be aware in advance of all five of these elements. Indeed rulers almost invariably underestimate how much they are seen as unjust or how much they have alienated elites; even if they have a sense that things are amiss and embark on reforms they frequently make things worse. Revolutionaries often underestimate the fiscal weakness of the old regime or the magnitude of popular support for the opposition. They may believe they are in a struggle that will still last for years when elites and the military defect and the old regime suddenly collapses. That is why even though revolutions may seem inevitable in hindsight, they are usually seen as unlikely, even unimaginable, right up to the moment they actually occur.

Structural and transient causes of revolutions

These five conditions together constitute an unstable equilibrium. Yet they are not causes—they do not explain what caused the social order to fray at so many levels all at once. We still have to ask what kinds of events will produce a combination of fiscal decay, elite alienation, popular anger at injustice, the spread of narratives of resistance, and international support for revolutionary change.

Scholars typically differentiate between structural and transient causes. Structural causes are long-term and large-scale trends that undermine existing social institutions and relationships. Transient causes are contingent events, or actions by particular individuals or groups, that reveal the impact of longer term trends and often galvanize revolutionary oppositions to take further action.

One very common structural cause of revolutions is demographic change. For most of history, population has changed very slowly or has grown more slowly than economic and technical progress. Under those conditions, direct inheritance provides a very secure way of replacing rulers, reconstituting elites, and even assigning ordinary people to their jobs or professions. Yet when the population grows rapidly for several generations, the cumulating effects of population change can cause the institutions of social order to suffer. Land and jobs may grow scarce; rents rise and real wages decline, producing popular anger. Prices will rise but taxes may lag, making it more difficult for the ruler to reward supporters and pay the troops. As elites have more surviving children, inheritance no longer provides for them all, and competition for elite positions heats up. Finally, sustained population growth produces ever-larger youth cohorts—often described as a "youth bulge"—who find difficulty obtaining suitable jobs and are easily drawn to new ideologies and mobilized for social protest.

A second common structural cause is a shift in the pattern of international relations. Wars and international economic competition can weaken state authorities and empower new groups in society. Revolutions frequently arose in waves following global or continental wars, as happened in Europe after the Thirty Years War, in the decades after the Napoleonic Wars, in the wake of World Wars I and II, and at the conclusion of the Cold War.

Changing population patterns and shifts in international relations often affect many states in a region at the same time, creating a large number of states that are simultaneously moving into unstable equilibrium. If a triggering event occurs in one such state, then the outburst of revolution in that state can itself serve as the triggering event for revolutionary outbreaks in others. This is why revolutions have frequently occurred in waves that seem to spread rapidly from one apparently stable country to the next.

A third structural cause is uneven or dependent economic development. It is normal for economic development to initially create more equality as some regions or groups benefit most from the new technologies or economic organization. But all groups should benefit to some degree, and the laggards usually catch up as the new technology and economic patterns spread. Where economic growth is so uneven that the poor and even middle classes fall farther behind while a small elite grows rapidly richer, or where economic growth is so dependent on foreign investment that growth benefits mainly the foreign investors and their associates, then economic changes will be widely seen as unjust, creating popular grievances, and alienating and dividing the elites.

A fourth and related structural cause is new patterns of exclusion or discrimination against particular groups. Inequality is universal in human societies. However, ambitious individuals aspire to improve their own positions by military, educational, or economic achievements, and most societies allow for a certain amount of mobility to absorb talented newcomers into the elite.

Where entire groups face legal discrimination—such as commoners in societies with hereditary nobles, or ethnic or religious minorities that are excluded from politics and certain economic roles—the discrimination must be well established and consistent to be accepted as part of the normal order.

By contrast, new or differently enforced discrimination or exclusion can undermine the legitimacy of a regime and turn entire groups into enemies of the existing social order. If existing channels of social mobility are suddenly blocked, if new groups take power and exclude former elites, or if the numbers and wealth of a group increase greatly without any increased political opportunities for that group, then the existing equilibrium becomes unstable, as an entire social group becomes aggrieved and seeks to change the social system that they believe is unjustly holding them down.

A fifth structural cause is the evolution of personalist regimes. In many countries a leader who has come to power through an election, or as the head of a military regime or a party-state, becomes increasingly entrenched over time. By manipulating elites and political institutions to stay in power decade after decade, the ruler comes to see himself as the indispensable leader of the nation. Such rulers typically weaken or alienate the regular professional military and business elites, relying more and more on a small circle of family and cronies who obtain high positions and great wealth through personal favor. What had been an elected, military, or party-based regime now becomes a personalist dictatorship.

In such regimes, the longer the ruler remains in power the more corrupt their regime becomes, as family members and cronies take greater advantage of their positions. The ruler may lose touch and not care whether the bulk of the population suffers from his economic policies. As more elite and popular groups feel excluded and estranged, they come to view the regime as illegitimate and unjust. Should a public protest, economic crisis, or particularly offensive action by the ruler spur revolt, such rulers may quickly find themselves isolated and deserted by their elites.

Both personalist dictators and traditional monarchies often fall victim to the combination of structural causes known as "the dictator's dilemma." The ruler of a relatively poor or backward nation often must invest heavily in upgrading its military and economic capacity to keep up with military and economic pressures from more advanced states. Doing so requires creating a more educated and professional military and civil service, encouraging private enterprise, increasing enrollments in schools and universities, and expanding cities and communications. It may also involve inviting extensive foreign investment.

But unless these processes are carefully managed, they can cause social relationships to fray. Better educated professionals, students, and private businessmen will resent the power and favoritism of a venal dictator, the privileges of entrenched elites, and the benefits going to foreign interests. Older elites may try to block the progress of newcomers. Growing private enterprises may displace peasants from their lands and compete with traditional craft workers. Expanded urban populations are more difficult to control and become centers for the spread of alternative ideologies. Modernizing dictatorships and monarchies thus lay the basis for a vigorous opposition to their rule; if they falter in the face of war or economic crises, or have fallen into patterns of blatant corruption and exclusionary rule, they are ripe for revolution.

In contrast to these structural causes, which gradually create unstable equilibrium over years or decades, transient causes are sudden events that push a society out of stability. These may include spikes in inflation, particularly of food prices; defeat in war; and riots or demonstrations that challenge state authority. In addition, state responses to protest can trigger wider protests.

When most people see protesters as extremists and they are isolated targets of state action, repression is usually effective. But when protesters are seen as ordinary members of society, then repression that is too broad or inconsistent can inflame elite and popular perceptions of the regime as dangerous, illegitimate, and unjust.

These transient events are indeed causes of revolutions, since in unstable states they lead people to turn against the state more openly and in larger numbers, or weaken the state's ability to defend itself and hasten elite defections. Yet the very same events occur in dozens of states each year without producing revolutions, because those states have the resilience to restore social order in the face of crises. It is therefore the interplay between actions and events and structural changes that give rise to revolutions.

Once a regime has been weakened, key elites have defected, and revolutionaries at the head of armies or popular revolts have seized power, a revolution has begun. Yet how events will end is still undetermined, for revolutions are long processes, not simple events. They may veer through counterrevolution, civil war, terror, and renewed revolutionary episodes before achieving stability. And their outcomes may range from democracy to renewed dictatorship.

Chapter 3
Revolutionary processes, leaders, and outcomes

Types of revolution

Societies differ in many ways. They may be ruled by monarchies, military dictatorships, party-states, or democratic governments. The population may be very large or quite small, mainly urban or largely rural, and very young (average age under twenty-five) or considerably older. Societies may be major powers in the international system, smaller states, or colonies of other powers. And, of course, societies differ greatly in their wealth and technology.

All these differences and others shape the possibilities and processes of revolutions. While the basic patterns of state weakness, elite divisions, popular grievances, narratives of injustice, and international engagement appear in revolutions throughout history, the resources available to states and their opponents, the kinds of elites and their privileges, the particular narratives of injustice and goals for change, and the tactics and patterns of popular mobilization vary. These differences have produced many types of revolutions.

Revolutions are often described in terms of their major goals. Those that mainly aim to change the type of regime are *political revolutions*. Revolutions that seek not only to change the regime, but also to dislodge a dominant social class from its status and property are *social revolutions*. The social revolutions that rocked major world powers are the most famous of all revolutions—known as the "Great Social Revolutions," these are the French Revolution of 1789, the Russian Revolution of 1917, and the Chinese Communist Revolution of 1949.

Political revolutions have had diverse goals. Some have aimed to replace a monarchy or dictatorship with a republic; these are often called "constitutional" revolutions. Others have sought to replace the existing government with a communist party-state or with religiously qualified leaders, producing "communist" or "religious" revolutions. Even democracies can be targeted: several have been overturned by mass mobilization to support fascist dictatorships, creating "fascist" revolutions. Finally, where a population was mobilized by local leaders to throw off the rule of a foreign power and create a new sovereign state, we see "anticolonial revolutions."

Revolutions are also distinguished by their tactics and settings. Revolutions that involve civil war or revolutionary terror (mass executions) are "violent revolutions." Revolutions driven mainly by peaceful occupation of city streets and squares are called "nonviolent," "urban," or sometimes "color" revolutions (named for the colored ribbons and banners that are typically used by protesters to identify themselves as opponents of the ruling regime.)

These different characteristics can combine to create varied patterns of revolutions. For example, anticolonial revolutions may be nonviolent (as with India's mobilization against British rule) or violent (such as the wars fought by Algeria and Vietnam against French rule). The Great Social Revolutions included both constitutional (French) and communist (Russia, China) revolutions. Constitutional revolutions have been won by leaders at the head of national armies (as in Turkey in 1923 or Japan in 1868) or at the head of peaceful crowds (as in the anticommunist revolutions in Eastern Europe in 1989).

27

Revolutions are therefore not a single type of event; revolutions form a genus with many species and subspecies.

The process of revolution

A revolution begins when the government loses control of a portion of its population and territory to groups demanding a change of government to rectify injustices. The area controlled by the opposition may be as small as a public square in a capital or regional city, or as distant as a mountain redoubt on the far edge of the country.

The process may begin with urban protests, workers' strikes, peasant uprisings, an elite challenge to the regime, or guerrilla attacks (or increasingly with social media campaigns). Indeed, some such actions may have been taking place for some time without any notable result. Most such beginnings lead to swift repression or years of futile and insignificant activity. However, if a country is already in unstable equilibrium, with the state facing economic or fiscal problems, a restive population, and declining loyalty among officials and elites, such events start to spread and reinforce each other, putting the regime on the defensive.

The government naturally tries to disperse the opposition but encounters surprising difficulty in doing so; its initial efforts at repression are followed by expanding demonstrations. The police are unable to cope with the growing disorders, and the government must call on the military for help. Yet the military turns out to be unreliable or ineffective.

This might be because soldiers or their officers have grievances of their own against the regime or because they identify with the protesters and are unwilling to fire on them. Key units may stand aside while others may even defect and go over to the opposition. The inaction of the military acts as a signal to the ruler, elites, and the population that the regime is defenseless. Crowds surge and take over the capital; similar mass demonstrations arise in other cities and the countryside. All of this generally unfolds over a few weeks or at most a few months. The ruler may then flee or be captured, while elites supported by crowds or the military take over government buildings and set up a provisional government.

But revolutions do not always triumph so quickly. In some cases, the revolutionary struggle takes years. If revolutionary leaders are unable to quickly build support in the cities, they may establish a foothold in some part of the country remote from the capital and government forces, usually in a mountainous or forested region, sometimes even just outside the country's borders. This rural base may remain small and insignificant for years. Yet if the regime is weakening economically, suffers military reversals, is losing legitimacy with popular groups, or is losing the loyalty of key elites, the opposition grows as it acquires new supporters, while support for the existing government declines. The rebels may adopt guerrilla warfare, melting into the countryside and striking periodically at government forces, or staging spectacular raids designed to demonstrate the weakness of the government. Workers may stage strikes in support of the rebels.

Eventually, the opposition may create a revolutionary army capable of fighting a civil war to take the capital city. Or the rebels may pursue nonviolent tactics using ever larger popular demonstrations, strikes, and boycotts to press the government to cede power. Either way, external powers may play a key role. If other nations help arm and organize the opposition, or if former external allies withdraw their support for the ruler, the balance of power can start to shift decisively in favor of the opposition. As the balance tips, government forces will suffer further declines in morale and military effectiveness. As the old regime's forces crumble or retreat, the revolutionary forces take the capital and establish a new regime.

In recent years, a third and novel pattern—the negotiated revolution—has emerged. These may start with mass demonstrations in the capital or the opposition gaining control of local bases. But instead of the ruler fleeing and ceding power to a provisional revolutionary government, or being driven out by a civil war, the authorities recognize that they cannot overcome the opposition and instead seek to negotiate the entry of the opposition into a new, joint regime. This may involve new elections in which both the ruling and opposition parties seek seats in the legislature, or joint councils with members of the opposition and the old regime leadership. However, the overwhelming popular support for the revolutionary party allows them to dominate the new institutions, win control of the government, and enact laws to reshape the political and economic order. Examples include the South African anti-apartheid revolution (which arose from bases in the Black townships) and the Polish Solidarity revolution (whose bases were in the shipyards and the Catholic Church).

Whether a revolutionary movement has pushed out the ruler with surprising speed in the capital, or advanced from a remote base in a lengthy struggle to displace the regime, or negotiated a transition of power, seizing power is just the first phase of the revolutionary process. Often the fall of the old regime is greeted with popular jubilation. A "revolutionary honeymoon" period of a few weeks ensues in which people exhibit enormous optimism for the future. If the revolution brought a constitutional regime, initial elections are greeted with great excitement and an outpouring of new parties and political groupings.

Yet critical questions need answers: How will government leaders be chosen and what laws will govern the exercise of power? Who will control the military? How will the new government finance its operations—by old taxes or new ones, by seizure of property or sale of state assets?

Other issues must also be settled. What will be the new regime's relations to other states—will it seek new allies or continue to fight the old regime's opponents? Will there be a change in the state religion? How will the remaining leaders and supporters of the old regime be treated? What new rules should guide the economy, education, the media, public services, or the role of minorities? And if the old regime was facing financial or military or economic crises, what measures will the new regime take to address them?

These questions are so wide-ranging and important that the diverse groups who made the revolution rarely agree on them. If the old regime's supporters have mostly fled and no pressing external threats are present, revolutionary leaders may be able to work out their differences peacefully, take the time to draft a constitution that can win wide support, and develop a sharing or alternation in power among different groups. But this is rare; more commonly disagreements over these pressing issues cause the revolutionary coalition to fracture. The revolution then enters the phase of postrevolutionary power struggles.

These struggles usually give rise to moderate and radical factions. Moderate factions may want to continue certain features or policies of the old regime and shrink from drastic changes in economic or social organization. Yet if war, economic crisis, or counterrevolution threatens the new regime, moderate measures often will not suffice. Should moderate policies fail, moderate leaders will be discredited and popular support will shift to radicals promising to bring better results by more extreme measures. Ruthless actions to raise revenues and military forces to defend the new regime, to redistribute property, and to deal with internal and external enemies become the order of the day.

These conflicts usually play out in ideological terms as well, with radical leaders claiming to be the "true voices" of the people and the revolution, while tarring moderates and opponents as reactionaries and traitors. New symbols and ceremonies, new forms of address (e.g., "citizen" and "comrade"), new official titles, new names for streets and cities, and new fashions in art and new

31

modes of dress (from the simple trousers of French *sans-culottes* to the women's headscarf [*hijab*] imposed in Iran) are commonly promoted by the new regime.

Radical groups often displace the moderates through a coup or insurrection, seizing power and taking over the revolutionary government. Demanding loyalty to their vision and policies, they may turn to purges or terror, executing and imprisoning many thousands. Often, revolutionaries will turn on each other, exiling or executing former comrades. Danton, Trotsky, Zapata, Lin Biao, Banisadr, and Escalante are just a few of the once-prominent revolutionary leaders who were sacrificed to the gods of revolution by their colleagues.

At some point, the radicals defeat their enemies or are defeated themselves. In many revolutions the political and economic disorder of the postrevolutionary power struggles invites a military or political leader to seize power and establish authoritarian rule, as with Oliver Cromwell, Napoleon, or Stalin. Once those leaders pass away or are defeated, however, the revolutionary regime may be overturned or may be put under the leadership of a more regular, bureaucratized regime. Whether it is the radicals and their heirs or moderate leaders who succeed to power, the postrevolutionary regime becomes the "new normal" government. People return to their normal routines rather than ideologically driven passions. After this phase of consolidation (which may take many years), things settle down and the revolution appears to be over.

Yet that may not be the end. After another decade or two, older radicals or a new generation may feel that this new order is failing to live up to the ideals of the revolution. They may seek to mobilize elite and popular groups for a new set of revolutionary measures, attacking existing officials and their policies, and seeking more radical economic and political changes. This second radical phase usually does not overturn the revolutionary government but revives its radicalism, which can lead to major policy shifts and new waves of popular mobilization and conflict. This second radical phase is usually the final burst of revolutionary energy; what follows is a reconsolidated, more stable version of the revolutionary regime. Examples of such "renewed radicalism" include Stalin's collectivization campaign in the 1930s, Mao's Cultural Revolution in the 1960s, and Lázaro Cárdenas's nationalizations and land reforms in Mexico in the 1930s.

The processes just described are commonly found in violent revolutions. These most often arise in countries with younger populations, because societies with large cohorts of young people are more likely to have significant groups who are drawn to radical ideologies and willing to engage in revolutionary violence. Revolutions that are nonviolent, or where moderates prevail and remain in power after the revolution, usually unfold in a different pattern of events, one more favorable to stability and constitutional government. We will discuss this trajectory below in our discussion of revolutionary outcomes.

Revolutionary leadership: visionary and organizational

Revolutionary leaders are the figures that embody revolutions. In their own countries, they may be revered as "fathers of the nation" and become the focus of personality cults. Some— Washington, Napoleon, Lenin—have gone down in history as heroes who created powerful new nations. Others—Robespierre, Stalin, Mao—are now often described as monsters who blindly pursued their ideologies and were responsible for the deaths of thousands or millions. To be accurate, many revolutionary leaders were a bit of both.

Because in hindsight the long-term and structural factors leading to revolution may seem overwhelming, the role of revolutionary leaders is sometimes minimized. When it seems that the old order was bound to collapse, revolutionary leaders simply emerge to pick up the pieces. Yet it requires skillful revolutionary leadership and tactics to take advantage of instability and disorder, to construct from this chaos a successful revolutionary movement, and to build a new regime. In the absence of revolutionary leaders who articulate and spread a new vision of society, an economic crisis or military defeat will likely be followed by the restoration of the old order with just a few institutional tweaks and adjustments. If revolutionary leaders are not able to weave together various elite and popular groups to build a durable coalition, the old regime will likely defeat its enemies and survive. The decisions to pursue moderate or radical policies, to enter into war or terror, and how to restructure law and society, as well as the ultimate success and outcomes of revolutions, are driven by revolutionary leaders.

Moderate revolutionary leaders are generally found within the ranks of the existing elite and often even within the existing regime. They may be military officers, politicians, officials, or other professionals. Frequently they are advocates of reform and only reluctantly pursue revolution when it appears that the old regime is too stubborn, too corrupt, or too incompetent to meet pressing challenges to the nation. Radical revolutionary leaders are also usually drawn from the ranks of the existing elites but from a more middling stratum of ambitious junior officers, professionals, university students, and local leaders. They generally have a radicalizing experience—they or a family member may have been abused by a government official, or they may have been punished for their political views. They tend to be fiercely patriotic and to have an unusually acute awareness of the problems in their society, thus devoting extensive time and effort to developing solutions and campaigning for major changes in government policies— campaigns that often get them into trouble with the authorities.

Revolutionary leadership requires two distinct kinds of skills. Visionary leaders are prolific writers, and often great speechmakers, who articulate the faults of the old society and make a powerful case for social change. They create a portrait of the injustices of the old regime and of the absolute necessity and inevitability of change that is capable of motivating and uniting diverse groups to support the revolution. During the revolution, visionary leaders continue to inspire and guide the revolutionary forces. Such visionary leaders include Thomas Jefferson, Robespierre, Francisco Madero, V. I. Lenin, Mao Zedong, Fidel Castro, Ho Chi Minh, Mahatma Gandhi, Václav Havel, and Ayatollah Khomeini.

Organizational leaders are great organizers and strategists; it is they who organize revolutionary armies and bureaucracies and make sure that they are paid and supplied. The organizational leaders figure out how to realize the ideas of visionary leaders, to make sure that the revolution can defeat its enemies and meet its economic and political goals. They tend to be pragmatic and are often skilled military generals. Such organizational leaders include George Washington, Napoleon, Venustiano Carranza, Leon Trotsky, Zhou Enlai, Raoul Castro, Vo Nguyen Giap, and Lech Wałęsa.

Successful revolutions require both kinds of leadership. Without visionary leaders to inspire and unite the opposition, the existing regime can usually isolate and defeat its fragmented opponents. Without organizational leaders, the revolutionary forces will easily be defeated by their opponents, either internal or external, as the new revolutionary regime fails because of ineffective policies and a lack of resources.

Most revolutions exhibit visionary and organizational leaders operating as partners; indeed they may have several leaders taking visionary and organizational roles. But in some cases, a single figure acts as both the visionary and organizational leader; notable examples include Simon Bolivar and Kemal Atäturk. Whatever their role, how revolutionary leaders are viewed is often determined by the outcomes of the revolutions they led.

Revolutionary outcomes

It is often difficult to determine the outcome of a revolution, as it is hard to know when the outcome should be assessed. Was the major outcome of the Russian Revolution of 1917 the deaths of millions of peasants who were killed in Stalin's collectivization campaigns of the 1930s? Or should we focus on the remarkable survival of the Soviet Union after the Nazi onslaught and its rise to become one of the world's two superpowers by the 1960s? Is the outcome of the American Revolution of 1776 the Constitution adopted in 1787, which has lasted for more than two hundred years? Or was the outcome of the revolution and the compromises in the Constitution the collapse of the United States into a bloody civil war over slavery in the 1860s?

The outcomes of revolutions are many and varied, and appear on different timescales. The American Revolution is hailed for creating a democracy; yet in fact more than half the population (women and slaves) was denied the vote for more than a hundred years. At the time of the Proletarian Cultural Revolution, China seemed to be torn apart and impoverished by internal conflict and ideological discord; twenty years later China was well on its way to achieving a modern miracle of growth and becoming the world's second largest economy.

Despite this variety, there are a few established principles regarding revolutionary outcomes. First, outcomes do not emerge quickly. The revolutionary processes described above typically take years or even decades to unfold. Ten to twelve years is the average time from the fall of the old regime until the features of the new postrevolutionary regime become clear.

Second, revolutions fall into several types with characteristic outcomes. Social revolutions involve the redistribution of large amounts of property and empower a revolutionary elite that pursues radical domestic and often foreign policies. Because of the great changes involved, they invariably invite efforts at counterrevolution and require a powerful regime to defend and consolidate the revolution. They therefore produce highly centralized, authoritarian states, often party-states or communist regimes, that are quite durable. They generally introduce social programs, such as land redistribution or collectivization, literacy and educational reforms, and public health measures aimed at establishing greater economic equality. They often experience a burst of rapid industrialization and economic growth due to the strong direction of the central regime, but this growth weakens and gives way to economic stagnation unless market-oriented reforms are introduced. Examples include the French, Mexican, Russian, Chinese Communist, Cuban, Ethiopian, and Iranian Islamic Revolutions.

Nonviolent urban revolutions seek to overturn an authoritarian regime that has grown corrupt, ineffective, and illegitimate and replace it with a more accountable and representative regime. Because they are nonviolent, they usually do not lead to a radical phase or to revolutionary terror, although war may break out after the old regime falls, because of either a power struggle among regions or groups or foreign intervention. If the revolution succeeds in forcing out the corrupt ruler, the government usually passes into the hands of a mixture of groups, none of which wishes to take the ruthless measures necessary to consolidate power and strengthen the new regime. These revolutions often drift; leaders fall into corruption and infighting. The eventual outcome is usually a flawed democracy with either frequent shifts in leadership or recurrent authoritarian tendencies. This is especially true when countries lack previous experience with democracy. Examples include the European Revolutions of 1848; the Chinese Republican Revolution of 1911; the anticommunist revolution in the Soviet Union; the "color revolutions" in Ukraine, the Philippines, and Georgia; and the 2011 Arab Revolutions in Tunisia and Egypt.

Not all revolutions fall into one of these major types. The 2011 Revolutions in Libya and Syria, for example, began as nonviolent urban revolutions but the tenacity of ethnic or tribal loyalties to the rulers led to civil war. The Turkish Revolution, the Japanese Meiji Restoration, and the Nasser Revolution in Egypt all sought to replace traditional monarchies or empires with modern national states with constitutions and secular governments; but all eventually led to military regimes. Of course, in some cases—from the American Revolution of the eighteenth century to the anticommunist revolutions in Eastern Europe in the twentieth—where moderate leaders prevailed and elites remained united, revolutions have created stable democratic regimes.

Third, while revolutions are made in the name of correcting injustice, concepts of "justice" may be narrow and harsh. When revolutions are made in the name of elevating a particular ideology, religion, or ethnic identity, this often makes new revolutionary regimes particularly harsh on minorities, who are scapegoated for social problems and singled out as traitors or enemies of the new regime. In some cases, such as the Nazi Revolution in Germany and the Khmer Revolution in Cambodia, assaults by the new regime on minorities reached the level of genocide. Racial and religious minorities may be promised much, but postrevolutionary societies rarely deliver true equality. For example, despite the U.S. Declaration of Independence proclaiming that "all men are created equal," in practice, long after the revolution this applied only to White Protestant men.

Fourth, another area in which revolutionary outcomes have consistently disappointed their followers is women's rights. Throughout history, women have marched, demonstrated, and fought alongside men for social justice. In the French Revolution, the women of Paris marched on Versailles to demand food for their families and children, and Marie Gouze published the *Declaration of the Rights of Woman*. In the Mexican Revolution, Dolores Jiménez y Muro and Hermila Galindo were leading political organizers and writers, while thousands of women fought as *soldaderas* in the revolutionary armies. In Russia and Germany, Alexandra Kollontai, Nadezhda Krupskaya, and Rosa Luxemburg helped lead the communist and socialist parties. In the Cuban Revolution, Celia Sánchez and Vilma Espín played key roles as strategists and fighters; the latter was a devoted champion for women's rights. In the Nicaraguan Revolution more than 30 percent of the armed Sandinistas were women.

In return for their courage and sacrifices, revolutionary leaders frequently promise equal roles for women in the new revolutionary regime. Yet without exception to date, once the revolutionary regime takes power, men seize most of the major political, military, and economic leadership posts, while women are encouraged to return to their homes and families. Even where women are given opportunities to gain an education, work, and enter the professions, they remain underpaid yet still bear the main burden for raising children and maintaining homes. While in a few cases women have emerged from revolutions as the leaders of their nation (such as Indira Gandhi in India, Violeta Chamorro in Nicaragua, and Corazon Aquino in the Philippines), this has only been as the heirs of politically prominent fathers or husbands. Alongside ethnic and religious minorities, women have consistently been let down by revolutionary promises for equality. Progress has come only when women have undertaken their own mass campaigns for gender equality.

Finally, revolutionary outcomes also impact the international order. We commonly identify revolutions by the name of a single country, such as the "French" or "American" or "Egyptian" revolutions. Yet revolutions are inherently transnational in both their origins and their outcomes. Revolutionary ideologies—whether constitutionalism or communism or radical Islamism—are often imported. Revolutionary leaders frequently seek inspiration, education, and support in foreign countries. And after arising in one nation, revolutions often set off waves of revolution that spread across entire regions.

The conditions that make states vulnerable to revolutions are themselves often transnational. Along with shifts in great power relations that affect entire regions, uneven economic development, population surges, unemployment, price spikes, and even corruption can take on a common pattern across neighboring regimes. A common narrative of injustice can thus spread across borders, even as it is adapted to specific countries. The outbreak of revolution in one country may trigger revolutions in others, as those seeking regime change take inspiration and hope (and learn tactics) from the initial case. Notable waves of revolution include the Revolutions of 1848 in Europe, the anticommunist revolutions of 1989–91 in Eastern Europe and the Soviet Union, and the Arab Revolutions of 2010–11.

Revolutions also commonly lead to international wars. Revolutionary regimes may seek new allies or identify new enemies, and they may try to spread their ideology and spur regime change in other countries. Countries may also feel threatened simply by the appearance of a new revolutionary regime, seeing it as a threat to the existing international order or as a model for rebellion in their own state. They may then strive to halt the contagion or reverse the revolution by military action. Notable postrevolutionary wars include the Napoleonic Wars after the French Revolution, the Iran–Iraq War after the Iranian Islamic Revolution, and the Russo-Ukrainian War following Ukraine's Maidan Revolution.

As we look across history, the costs of revolutions have been stark—in the French Revolution more than a million French men and women died in the civil and international wars that followed, roughly one in twenty of the prerevolutionary population. Tens of millions perished as a result of the Mexican, Russian, and Chinese Communist Revolutions, roughly one in ten of these countries' peoples. The Fascist and Nazi Revolutions in Europe launched World War II, and the Khmer Rouge Revolution in Cambodia killed nearly 30 percent of the population in war and genocide.

Several of the Arab Revolutions of 2011—in Libya, Syria, and Yemen—launched a decade and more of civil war. Revolutions thus deserve their reputation for bringing horror as well as heroism.

Yet in recent decades, violent social revolutions have been fewer, while nonviolent urban revolutions have grown far more common, becoming the dominant form of revolutionary struggle. As societies have become more urbanized, and middle-income and more developed societies have gained older populations, the number of nonviolent urban revolutions has grown. Moreover, these nonviolent revolutions have proven far more successful than violent revolutions in both changing regimes and creating stable democracies. While world history bears the scars of violent revolutions, without revolutions we would not have today's democratic and constitutional governments or our concepts of citizenship and human rights. As the types and processes of revolution continue to evolve (today we find both revolutionary organization and state coercion carried out in cyberspace), we may hope that the noble goals of revolutions may be grasped without the enormous costs of past bloodshed.

Chapter 4
Revolutions in the ancient world

Revolutions are nearly as old as history itself. Ever since we have had records of government and taxation—as long ago as the pharaohs of Egypt—there have been efforts to overthrow governments in the name of greater social justice and to replace one set of government institutions with different ones.

Revolutions from the pharaohs to Greece and Rome

The reign of Pepi II, the last pharaoh of the Old Kingdom in Egypt, appears to have ended in a revolution in the twenty-second century BCE. The pharaoh was losing control to regional lords, and as central rule weakened, people attacked the homes of the wealthy and seized their possessions. Magistrates were driven from their offices and palaces plundered. An ancient papyrus scroll describing this event relates how amid famine and destruction, the social order was overturned: "The poor man is full of joy. Every town says: 'Let us suppress the powerful among us.'... The son of a man of rank is no longer distinguished from him who has no such father.... Behold, the possessors of robes are [now] in rags [while] He who begged for himself his dregs [has] bowls full to overflowing.... The King has been taken away by poor men." Local oligarchies took over and ruled for more than a hundred years, until a new pharaoh established the first dynasty of the Middle Kingdom. During the Egyptian revolution of 2011, Egyptians proudly retold this story of the world's first known popular revolution to show that Egyptians had a long history of challenging injustice.

Archeologists have also found evidence of attacks on palaces in the eastern Mediterranean in the thirteenth century BCE, but it is uncertain whether these were marauders or revolutions. However, by the eighth century BCE in Greece, we find indisputable cases of conflict leading to constitutional changes.

Up to about 800 BCE, the cost of bronze arms and chariots was so great that only aristocrats could afford them. Kings backed by aristocrats and priests were dominant. Indeed in Egypt, Persia, and elsewhere, rulers claimed divine or semidivine status. Popular mobilization to change the nature of government was quite rare.

As populations grew, trade increased and weapons became more affordable. Heavily armed infantry (hoplites) replaced aristocratic charioteers as the core of armies. This undermined the aristocrats' dominance, and Greek societies began to experience organized conflict between elite and popular groups. These conflicts produced periodic shifts in power, several of which led to major changes in government institutions. For the first time in history, from roughly 700 BCE to 100 CE, revolutions became fairly common.

The ancient Greeks observed their city-states undergoing many changes of regime, from monarchy to tyranny and from aristocracy to democracy, and wrote extensively about revolutions. For both Plato and Aristotle, the primary cause of revolutions was social injustice. Plato argued that the best society is ruled by an aristocracy based on merit and virtue; but when aristocracies focus on money instead of virtue, they become selfish, rival-torn oligarchies (governments run by and for the wealthy) and will be overthrown by the people. The latter would create a democracy;

but a democracy in turn is likely to degenerate as everyone pursues their own interests. Eventually this disorder opens the way for a tyrant to seize power. Aristotle identified many different causes that could lead to revolution, including personal rivalries and external interventions. But the primary cause was always injustice—either the wealthy few oppressing the poorer majority or the poorer majority making attacks on the rich. For Aristotle stability depended on having a constitution that maintained a balance of wealth and population, with no citizens too rich or too poor.

Many Greek city-states underwent a series of revolutions as popular and oligarchic factions fought for power. These revolutions often arose in the wake of wars, particularly when military defeat weakened the ruling party. A common pattern was for aristocrats to be overthrown by a populist leader who became a tyrant. Then the tyrant would be overthrown by a popular movement, which produced a formal constitution, seeking to create a more balanced, law-based form of government. The constitutions of Solon for Athens and of Lycurgus for Sparta were the best-known models, both relying on an assembly of male citizens to make the laws.

During the Peloponnesian Wars, when Athens and Sparta vied for power across Greece, they often fomented revolutions, seeking to overturn governments allied to their rival (much like the United States and the Soviet Union during the modern Cold War). The great ancient historian of these wars, Thucydides, showed how much of Greece was convulsed by revolutions in this period. In Book 3 of *The History of the Peloponnesian War* he describes in detail the revolution in Corcyra (427 BCE), in which the pro-Athenian democratic faction (which freed the slaves to fight on their behalf) fought against the pro-Spartan oligarchic faction (which hired mercenaries to fight for them). Thucydides reports that much like the great revolutions that came in later centuries, the revolution in Corcyra was characterized by butchery and chaos—"Death thus raged in every shape, and as usually happens at such times, there was no length to which violence did not go." The revolt ended when Athens sent a large fleet to Corcyra, and the democratic faction massacred its rivals.

The glories of Rome also have their roots in an ancient revolution. It appears that the city-state of Rome was initially ruled by foreign Etruscan kings. At the end of the sixth century BCE the Romans rose up and expelled the last foreign king, replacing the monarchy with a citizen-based government, which they called a republic. This term came from the Latin "res publica" or "public affairs," indicating that politics were now a public concern, not a private matter for kings and nobles. This revolution produced a regime in which an aristocratic Senate advised the state and proposed laws, but all citizens voted in assemblies that elected the major officials—the consuls and tribunes—and passed the laws.

The Roman Republic lasted roughly five hundred years in this form. But as the Republic's conquests grew, and the population and land under control of the city increased, it became more difficult for the institutions designed for citizens to participate in government to function. Immense wealth accrued to the leading senators and immense power to leaders of the army. The Senate had increasing difficulty controlling the leading generals, and the people lost faith in the Senate. In the late second century BCE the Gracchus brothers, Tiberius and Gaius, who were tribunes elected by the Plebian Council, tried to pass laws that would redistribute some of the wealth of the patricians to the common people. Sometimes lauded as history's first socialists, they were assassinated for their troubles, and their efforts failed.

The leading generals then sought to win popular support for their challenges to the Senate. In 49 BCE, after a series of military victories abroad that gained him great fame and popularity, Julius Caesar defied the Senate's attempt to relieve him of his command and instead took his army to Rome. He spent the next five years

1. The Roman Senate, consisting of wealthy citizens and former magistrates, chose the officials of the Roman Republic and advised them on policy. This nineteenth-century painting shows the orator Marcus Tullius Cicero in the first century BC addressing the Senate.

warring against his opponents, conquering Egypt (and its queen, Cleopatra), and having the Senate grant him more extensive and permanent powers. In 44 BCE, as told by Plutarch and Shakespeare, he was assassinated by a group of senators who feared his growing power.

After his death, his nephew Octavian, drawing on the enormous popularity of Caesar with the people and soldiers of Rome, undertook a series of civil wars to defeat all of his uncle's enemies. When Octavian gained sole power, in what is now commonly called "The Roman Revolution," he completed the work of degrading the powers of the Senate and Assemblies, and created the political framework for the Roman Empire.

Octavian adopted the name Augustus Caesar. Although he permitted the Senate and Assemblies to exist, he increasingly had himself portrayed as having divine attributes, thus putting his decisions above any other laws or institutions. He took control of the selection of military and civilian officials, placing trusted kin and loyalists in key positions. The new imperial system lay the groundwork for almost two thousand years in which all Roman emperors, Byzantine emperors, and later the kings of Europe would claim a "divine right" to rule.

The Roman religion at the time of Augustus followed the Greeks in having many gods, so that taking on divine attributes made Augustus just another one of the many descendants of the Olympians who had been heroes or demigods on earth. However, when Christianity came to the empire, the one true God and His son, Jesus Christ, were considered to have given their divine authority to kings to rule over humanity as their earthly regents. This placed kings above any manmade laws and made rebellion against a duly-anointed king an act of heresy, not merely political conflict. As a result, people became subjects rather than citizens, and revolutions went into abeyance for more than a thousand years.

Revolutions in abeyance under emperors and kings, 1 CE–1200 CE

Ancient Greece and Italy were not rich areas—mountainous and swampy peninsulas, they lacked the vast river valleys and plains that had been the foundation for wealthy empires in Egypt, Mesopotamia, Persia, northern India, and China. Whereas the city-states of Greece and Rome thus developed as small, fairly egalitarian societies that experienced revolutions and developed constitutions and the concept of citizenship, no similar developments took place in other major civilizations. Indeed, wherever vast empires arose, government took the form of a divinely sanctioned hereditary ruler wielding enormous wealth and power through an appointed bureaucracy of powerful officials, usually in close cooperation with a hierarchy of religious priests. Such bureaucratic-agrarian empires often experienced peasant uprisings and regional rebellions, but underwent dynastic cycles rather than experiencing revolutions.

In these empires, a ruling family would periodically encounter difficulty maintaining their rule. As with Pepi II, local lords might gain power at the expense of the central regime. Or the overall economy would experience a period of difficulty due to sustained population increase; the resulting scarcity of land would make it more difficult for peasants to feed their families, and for elites and the imperial government to sustain their revenues. Elites then would call for reform and would usually claim that an unjust ruler was responsible for their ills. Yet such empires generally held to an ideal of a golden past associated with the founding era or sacred books of their civilization. So when injustice, popular suffering, and administrative crises arose, the diagnosis was always that the ruler had departed from the traditional virtues of the past. In China, the phrase was that the ruler had "lost the mandate of Heaven" for failing to conform to Confucian virtues. An uprising against the government that produced a new ruler therefore usually led to administrative reforms designed to make the new government a more efficient version of the older, idealized model. A new dynasty would thus arise, but its political institutions would simply be a somewhat reformed version of those of the previous regime.

This was the pattern that prevailed in the Hellenistic kingdoms, which arose in the eastern Mediterranean and central Asia after Philip of Macedon and Alexander the Great had extinguished the independence of the Greek city-states and created a vast empire. It was the pattern in Islamic civilization, including Persia, the Arab caliphate, and the Islamic dynasties of North Africa and Spain, and the Turkish Ottoman Empire. Indeed, the fourteenth-century Arab sociologist Ibn Khaldun was the first scholar to detail a theory of dynastic cycles. It was also the pattern of classical India, of the Byzantine Empire in the eastern Mediterranean, and of Imperial China. And it also became the pattern in Europe under the Roman Empire from the time of Augustus.

There were a few exceptions wherein a shift of dynastic control from one ruling family to another did have the character of a revolution, with a fight for greater justice producing a new pattern of regime authority or new groups rising to power. Two of these still influence modern-day politics.

One was the struggle in the early Islamic Empire known as the "Abbasid Revolution." After the death of the Prophet Muhammad in 632 CE, his followers chose the head of the Muslim community, the caliph. Under the early caliphs, Islam spread across the Middle East. The fourth caliph was Ali, Muhammad's first cousin and son-in-law, and closest living relative. However, in 661 CE Ali was assassinated. After his death, power was claimed by the governor of Syria, who founded the Umayyad dynasty. Over the next century, the Umayyad caliphs expanded Islamic control from Spain to Persia. Yet they faced many revolts, most notably by the followers of Ali. These partisans (in Arabic, *shi'a*) of Ali claimed that the caliphate should remain in direct descent from the prophet, and thus that the Umayyad caliphs were not legitimate. Ali's younger son, Hussein ibn Ali, led a rebellion against the Umayyads, but in 680 CE Hussein was defeated and killed at the battle of Karbala.

Nonetheless, the Umayyads faced further challenges. Despite the vast expansion of their empire, they continued to privilege Arabs and especially Syrians, treating non-Arab converts as second-class Muslims and barring them from official posts. They raised taxes to extreme levels and were accused of impious behavior. Popular opposition to Umayyad rule grew steadily, centered on more zealous Muslims who wanted to return the caliphate to a descendant of the prophet and who also offered to treat all Muslims, especially Persian converts, as equals. Raising a military force in Persia, the followers of Abu al-Abbas (who claimed

49

descent from the prophet through an uncle) defeated the Umayyads in 750 CE. Upon taking power, the new ruler shifted the capital from Damascus in Syria to Baghdad, where the Abbasid caliphs ruled for five hundred years, presiding over the fusion of Arabic and Persian culture that produced the Islamic Golden Age. A remnant of the Umayyads fled to Spain, where they established a rival caliphate in Cordoba.

The Abbasids' treatment of all Muslims who recognized the caliphate as equals was a social revolution, and persisted through the centuries up through the rule of the Ottoman Empire, which claimed the caliphate in the fifteenth century and moved it to Istanbul. All those who recognized the authority of the Abbasid and later Ottoman caliphate were known as Sunni Muslims. Yet a considerable fraction of Muslims did not recognize the Abbasid claim of descent from the prophet and continued to look for a savior and future caliph from the line of Ali. They are known as Shi'a Muslims and still commemorate Hussein's martyrdom at the battle of Karbala on the holiday of Ashura. In the sixteenth century the Safavid dynasty in Iran, seeking to justify its claims to power against its Ottoman rivals, adopted Shi'a as their official religion, producing a fusion of Iranian nationalism with the Shi'a faith. Conflict between Sunni and Shi'a Muslims continues to shape politics in the Middle East and North Africa to this day, influencing modern revolutionary movements in Bahrain, Iran, Iraq, Lebanon, Syria, and other nations.

Another early revolution with modern reverberations was the Maccabean Revolution in 164 BCE. After the death of Alexander the Great, the Jewish lands of Palestine had come under the control of a Syrian dynasty, the Seleucids. The Seleucid rulers promoted the Greek religion and culture, which was attractive even to many Jews, so that the Jewish leadership grew divided between those accepting Greek customs and fundamentalists who urged strict adherence to traditional Jewish law. In 167 BCE the Seleucid King Antiochus IV sought to end

Jewish practices and enforce Greek laws and worship; he outlawed temple sacrifices, circumcision, observance of the Sabbath and Jewish holidays, public readings of the Torah, and sought to establish the worship of pagan gods in the Jewish temple. Some Jews, citing the might of Antiochus, went along with the changes. Others accepted execution rather than give up their traditional ways. But one group, led by the Jewish priest Mattathias and his sons in a village outside of Jerusalem, called themselves "Maccabees" (the hammer) and resolved to fight to restore Jewish worship and throw off Seleucid rule.

Their story reads like a modern revolution. The Maccabees began with guerrilla warfare against the Seleucid forces; building on early success they then raised a conventional army under the leadership of Mattathias's son Judah and his brothers. They developed a visionary ideology of opposition based on the book of Daniel and presented Judah as a modern version of the biblical Joshua who had liberated Canaan. Relying on superior zeal and tactics, they repeatedly defeated much larger military forces sent against them by the Seleucids; they also adroitly exploited divisions in the Seleucid leadership and benefitted from alliances with Sparta and Rome.

In 164 BCE, the Maccabees captured Jerusalem and celebrated by purifying the temple of all pagan cults and lighting the temple flame, which by legend burned for eight days on only a day's worth of oil. Fighting continued on and off for another twenty-three years until the last Syrian garrison was finally expelled. The Maccabees established a new Jewish dynasty in Palestine, imposed circumcision and other Jewish laws, and expanded their kingdom to include all of what is today modern Israel north of the Negev desert. To this day, Jews celebrate these events with the Festival of Lights, known as Chanukah, and the Maccabean Revolution inspires Jewish efforts to preserve an independent state of Israel. After several generations, though, Jewish independence was ended by the Romans, whose general Pompey invaded and took control of Israel in 63 BCE.

After the reign of Augustus, despite regional rebellions and civil wars among generals, and the division of the Roman Empire into Western (Latin) and Eastern (Greek) empires, there were no further revolutions for many centuries. The power of the Roman and Byzantine states, the quasi-divine status of the emperors, and the effectiveness of their legions prevailed against popular uprisings for more than a thousand years. Even after the Roman Empire in the West collapsed because of invasions by Frankish and Germanic tribes, when Charlemagne reestablished a large territorial empire in Europe spanning portions of France, Germany, and Italy, he claimed the mantle of Rome. In 800 CE he had himself crowned by the pope as Holy Roman Emperor, a title that his successors continued to claim up until the French Revolution.

When the German and French branches of Charlemagne's family empire separated, the German branch continued to claim the imperial title. Meanwhile, the kings of France and England also claimed divine right and indeed were thought to be endowed with certain divine powers, such as the ability to cure the skin disease of scrofula with the royal touch. Revolution as a mode of politics did not return to Western Europe until the rise of new city-states in Italy in the Renaissance and the spread of religious skepticism during the Enlightenment.

Chapter 5
Revolutions of the Renaissance and Reformation

After the breakup of Charlemagne's empire, three major powers—the king of France, the German Holy Roman Emperor, and the pope (who had established a growing territory in Italy)—dominated Europe. In the cracks between these empires, along a line from central Italy up through southern and central Germany and into the Low Countries, trading towns grew into commercial cities, with the strongest proclaiming themselves to be free city-states. The earliest and strongest of these arose in Northern Italy. In these cities, the growth of new commercial groups and their struggles with the older landed aristocracy over issues of religion and politics produced numerous revolutions.

Revolutions in Renaissance Italy

The Republic of Florence was founded in 1115, when the city rebelled against the Margrave of Tuscany. As the city grew richer, two major political factions developed: the Ghibellines who represented the landed aristocracy, and the Guelphs who were rich merchants and leaders of the major guilds. In 1250 the Guelphs drove the Ghibellines from power and forced the aristocrats to cut down their towers. Then in 1260, after a defeat by the neighboring city of Sienna, the Guelphs' rule was overturned and the Ghibellines returned to power. But this did not last either, as Ghibelline excesses stirred up popular uprisings, and papal intervention soon helped to restore the Guelphs.

In 1378 an uprising of the lower working classes led by the wool workers (the *ciompi*) overthrew the Guelphs. The workers stormed the prisons and state buildings, and declared a government by the people. The *ciompi* rule of Florence—perhaps the most democratic of this period—lasted almost three years before they were deposed by a party led by Salvestro de' Medici.

These class struggles faded in the early 1400s as the Medicis, who rose to wealth as bankers to the popes and gained immortal fame as magnificent patrons of Renaissance art, gradually took control of Florence. The Medicis dominated the Florentine Republic until 1494, when King Charles VIII of France invaded Italy. Piero de' Medici (known to history as "Piero the Unfortunate") humiliatingly capitulated to all of Charles's demands, and as a result was overthrown by Florence's most fanatical revolutionary leader, Girolamo Savonarola.

Savonarola was a Dominican friar and an early religious fundamentalist who wanted Florence to become a "city of God." He denounced clerical corruption and the exploitation of the poor. He ordered a "bonfire of the vanities," having ostentatious wigs, perfumes, paintings, and even ancient pagan manuscripts publicly burned. For four years Florence was ruled as a Christian commonwealth, with the Gospel as law, inspired by Savonarola's fiery preaching. Yet Savonarola went too far; his claims of prophecy brought him into conflict with the pope, who excommunicated him. As with many revolutionaries, people grew tired of living by extremes and turned on Savonarola. In 1498 his opponents took power and put Savonarola on trial for heresy and sedition. When his sentence was confirmed by the pope, the great preacher was hanged and burned in the public square.

2. Girolamo Savonarola, a fiery Dominican friar and preacher, briefly persuaded the citizens of Florence to overturn their government, put aside their finery and pursuit of wealth, and become a "city of God." However, he went too far in his prophecies and criticisms of all authorities and was eventually denounced and excommunicated by the pope. Savonarola met his end when, after being attacked by a Florentine mob, he was arrested on charges of heresy brought by papal commissioners. The city council ordered his execution, and he was tortured, hung, and burned in the Piazza della Signoria in 1498.

In the following decades, the Medicis returned to power in Florence and though briefly expelled by another popular revolt in 1527–30, eventually ended the republic, becoming Dukes of Florence and later Grand Dukes of Tuscany.

Although Florence was the site of the most frequent and extreme revolutions of this period, throughout Italy parties associated with elite or populist groups contested for power. Advantage frequently shifted, with the winning party sometimes supported by the pope, sometimes by the emperor. In fact, our modern word for "revolutions" comes from this period, when Italians began to refer to the frequent rotations of power between different groups as a *revolutio*, from the Latin "revolvere," to cycle or revolve.

Revolutions in the Reformation

Savonarola was not the only monk repelled by corruption among the clergy. In Germany, Martin Luther, a monk and professor of theology, issued a fundamental challenge to the corruption and earthly power of the pope. The resulting Reformation swept Europe, giving rise to Lutheran and other reform groups, who often challenged Catholic rulers for political control. Followers of John Calvin of Geneva in particular sought to create governments that were "godly" in virtue rather than subservient to the evils of the papacy. In several cases—including the Dutch Revolt against Spain in the 1560s and the English Revolution in the 1640s— Calvinists led political revolutions in the name of virtue.

The English Revolution was the first revolution in modern history to put a king on trial and formally execute him. In the late sixteenth and early seventeenth centuries, rapid population growth in England led to falling wages and a vast expansion of London. At the same time, rising prices and expenses led the Crown to sell lands and titles, creating an expanded and increasingly contentious elite. These elites, represented in Parliament, clashed with the king over matters of religion and taxation. By 1638 King Charles I had dismissed Parliament, expanded taxation by decree, imposed harsh and often arbitrary rule in Ireland, repressed English Calvinists (the Puritans), and, most foolishly, attempted to impose Anglican religious practices on Presbyterian Scotland. When the Scots raised an army to resist, Charles had to recall Parliament to ask for funds to respond.

From 1640 to 1642, Parliamentary leaders demanded ever greater concessions in return for granting funds. Yet Charles resisted any infringement on his powers. By the summer of 1642, as the power struggle intensified, Parliament had raised an army, drawing on the county militias and support from the City of London. To oppose them, Charles raised his standard at Nottingham in August and gathered an army of loyal royalists; the result was a series of civil wars.

56

Oliver Cromwell, a brilliant general known as "Old Ironsides," led the parliamentary forces to victory. Inspired by Puritan preachers, Cromwell and his army also sought to create a virtuous, godly state. After Charles was tried and executed in 1649, Cromwell became Lord Protector of the British Commonwealth. Under the Commonwealth, the House of Lords was abolished, as was the monarchy, and a Calvinist Church was established. In 1649 Parliament declared "that the people are, under God, the original of all just power; that the Commons of England, being chosen by and representing the people, have the supreme power in this nation."

But Cromwell too could not work with Parliament. Five months after his first Parliament met, Cromwell dissolved it and divided England into military districts, ruled by his chosen major-generals. After his death, people sought a return to normalcy, and in 1660 Charles's son was welcomed back to take the throne as Charles II. (Maybe not quite normalcy, for the Royalists did bear a grudge—they had Cromwell's body dug up from its grave in Westminster Abbey, hung in chains, and beheaded.)

The English Revolution and its aftermath inspired some of the most profound works of political theory in the English language, including John Milton's defense of free speech in *Areopagitica* (1644); Thomas Hobbes's argument for absolute sovereign authority, based on reason and the need to avoid civil violence, and one of the first works to study politics in terms of a social contract, in *Leviathan* (1651); and John Locke's defense of natural rights in *Two Treatises of Government* (1689).

Locke was one of the English leaders who contributed to what was perhaps the most significant revolution of this era, the "Glorious Revolution" of 1688–89. Britain had been a Protestant nation since Henry VIII's break with the papacy in the mid-1500s, with Anglicanism the official state religion and public Catholic worship illegal. Yet many Britons, including members of its royal family, remained adherents of the Roman Catholic faith. In 1685

Charles II died without children, and his Catholic brother became King James II. James sought to restore Catholic influence in Britain, reshaping the universities and appointing Catholics to leading positions in the government. Claiming divine right, he proclaimed that he had the right to dispense with any laws of Parliament he wished. Concerned about the growing Puritan colonies in North America, he revoked their charters and remodeled all the colonies of New England, plus New York and New Jersey, into a single Dominion of New England under a royal governor.

After a male heir was born to James and his queen in 1688, a group of British Protestant leaders, fearing that they would be saddled with a Catholic succession, offered their support to William of Orange, the Protestant ruler of Holland, if he would bring an army to England to depose James. William had married James's daughter Mary, and he was promised that if successful they could rule England together. Later that year, William landed a large invasion force in southern England. Faced with these forces and defections from his own officers, James fled to France. Parliament ruled that James had thereby abdicated and offered William and Mary the throne as king and queen.

But the true significance of this revolution lay in the Toleration Act and the Bill of Rights, which Parliament passed in 1689. The Bill of Rights determined that Parliament would set the rules for succession to the throne, and set limits on the powers of the crown in domestic affairs including prohibiting taxation without Parliamentary consent, prohibiting the King from keeping a standing army without such consent, and granting the rights of Protestants to hold arms. The Bill also established the rights of Parliament, including freedom of speech in Parliament and the requirement to hold free and regular parliamentary elections, and gave rights to subjects, including duly impaneled juries and a ban on excessive bail and on cruel and unusual punishments. The Toleration Act greatly expanded religious freedom. Although the act did not permit public worship by Catholics and allowed only

Anglicans to hold state offices and university positions, it ended the discord between the Anglican Church and the other major

From the English Bill of Rights (1689):

"for the vindicating and asserting their ancient rights and liberties declare:

- That the pretended power of suspending the laws or the execution of laws by regal authority without consent of Parliament is illegal;

- That the pretended power of dispensing with laws or the execution of laws by regal authority, as it hath been assumed and exercised of late, is illegal;

- That the commission for erecting the late Court of Commissioners for Ecclesiastical Causes, and all other commissions and courts of like nature, are illegal and pernicious;

- That levying money for or to the use of the Crown by pretense of prerogative, without grant of Parliament, for longer time, or in other manner than the same is or shall be granted, is illegal;

- That it is the right of the subjects to petition the king, and all commitments and prosecutions for such petitioning are illegal;

- That the raising or keeping a standing army within the kingdom in time of peace, unless it be with consent of Parliament, is against law;

- That the subjects which are Protestants may have arms for their defense suitable to their conditions and as allowed by law;

- That election of members of Parliament ought to be free;

(continued)

Protestant groups. The act gave all Protestant sects that accepted the Holy Trinity the right to worship openly and without penalty. This enabled Baptists, Presbyterians, Quakers, and Independents to take prominent roles in England's economy and society.

It is hard to overstress the importance of these acts. For the first time since Augustus, the divine right of kings had been explicitly denied, with laws passed by Parliament clearly elevated over the will of the king, indeed with Parliament declaring its right to bestow the Crown. After several centuries in which the power of kings in Europe had been growing, with monarchs like Louis XIV in France, Frederick William I of Brandenburg-Prussia, and Philip IV of Spain diminishing their local parliaments and developing absolutist rule, the rights of Parliament in Britain were definitively upheld. And in sharp opposition to the practice established in the Treaty of Westphalia in 1648 and carried out with increasing vigor in most of Europe, where monarchs were entitled to choose a state religion and enforce its practice on their subjects, the Act of Toleration guaranteed freedom of worship for certain groups of dissenters from the established Anglican Church. Although the revolutionaries claimed that they were simply restoring the historical balance of power between the king and Parliament, these acts in fact embodied many of the ideas that would be at the core of the revolutions to come in America and France in the following century.

Chapter 6
Constitutional revolutions: America, France, Europe (1830 and 1848), and Meiji Japan

From ancient times up until the eighteenth century, revolutionaries thought of themselves as fighting for justice and creating new regimes, but they did so in traditional terms. That is, they might seek to overthrow their king for being an unjust ruler, or to replace one national religion with another, or even to create a republic led by an assembly of notables or citizens. Yet they never fought against kingship or religion per se. They always relied on some form of state-supported religion and some elements of traditional customs or authority to maintain social order.

The most radical revolutions of the ancient world, those that created the city-states and constitutions of Athens, Sparta, Rome, and other republics, built on local custom and religion. The leader of England's Puritan Revolution, Oliver Cromwell, who led the execution of the king and the creation of a commonwealth, nonetheless spoke in 1654 to defend "the ranks and orders of men,—whereby England hath been known for hundreds of years....A nobleman, a gentleman, a yeoman; the distinction of these: that is a good interest of the nation, and a great one!" And the revolutionaries of 1688, who created what we now in retrospect call a constitutional monarchy—that is, a monarch bound by the laws of an elected parliament—had no idea or plan to create a constitution. Rather, they believed they were simply restoring the traditional balance in England between Crown and Parliament, ruling jointly, and they called their revolution "Glorious" because they believed it reestablished a golden order of the past.

The idea that a revolution is a fundamental break with the past, that revolutionaries can create something entirely new by force of will and frame a government using the principles of reason—not custom or religion—is something distinctly modern.

In the course of the seventeenth and eighteenth centuries, as scientific discoveries caused people to become skeptical about the truth of religious authority, and to put more faith in reason and practical experience, ideas about governance changed as well, with revolutionary implications. People began to doubt that rulers had a divine right to rule and instead started to see monarchy as simply an old custom that need not bind modern men. They also began to see churches as institutions that people created to choose their own ways to worship God, not divine institutions to which people owed complete obedience. This growing skepticism and secularism led to a modern twist in revolutions—revolutionaries that attacked the claims of kings and churches to lead society, and who drew up constitutions based on reason and the concept of natural rights to liberate men (though not yet women) from these authorities.

The American Revolution

The British colonies of North America were founded in the early 1600s by commercial companies and religious groups seeking freedom from British society: Puritans in New England, Quakers in Pennsylvania, Catholics in Maryland, and plantation colonies in Virginia. Yet all the colonies obtained charters from the British Crown, and although they elected their own local legislatures, they were still ruled by royal governors as subjects of the king. The colonies grew rapidly and prospered by trading tobacco, wheat, cotton, timber, and furs. As they pushed west into the Appalachians, British government forces played a key role in defeating the French and their Native American allies in the French and Indian War (1754–1763).

The war was expensive, and the British government was determined to recover its costs from the colonists by imposing a series of new taxes and constraints on trade and consumption. When the colonists refused to pay these new taxes (including a demonstration in which chests of British tea were dumped into Boston Harbor), sharp divisions arose between rebels and loyalists. While the latter supported British rule, many colonial elites, from Virginia plantation owners to New York and Boston bankers and lawyers, as well as popular groups, were outraged that they were being forced to pay for Britain's wars without any say or consent.

The American colonists believed they enjoyed the rights that Englishmen had won in the Revolution of 1688–89, to have a Parliament of their choosing agree to any taxes and to rule together with the king. By the 1770s many felt they were being ruled despotically by a faraway king and that their basic liberties were being stripped away. American orators made stirring speeches about rights and liberties. Perhaps the most famous was Patrick Henry's bold plea, as he persuaded his fellow Virginians to join the revolutionary cause: "Is life so dear, or peace so sweet, as to be purchased at the price of chains and slavery?...Give me liberty or give me death!"

Thomas Paine's pamphlet *Common Sense*, published in January 1776, argued that it was absurd for an island like Britain to claim to rule a continent like America; that all men were created equal and owed no allegiance to a distant king who had no interest in the welfare of Americans; and that America should hold a continental congress and draw up a charter of independence. In July, American leaders did just that, publishing the Declaration of Independence, drafted by Thomas Jefferson. The Declaration stated that King George III was an unjust king who had violated Americans' "self-evident...rights [to] Life, Liberty, and the pursuit of Happiness," and that the purpose of government was to secure these rights, "deriving their just powers from the consent of the governed."

This extraordinary claim—that the power of kings came not from God but that all governments should derive their power from consent of the governed—led to eight years of war with Britain, which sought to enforce its claims to royal rule. George Washington, appointed as head of the colonial army, brilliantly organized and shepherded the ragged colonial military through several years when mere survival was remarkable, withdrawing from the major cities but making daring raids and surprise attacks on British forces. Eventually, France decided that it could avenge its defeat in the French and Indian War by helping the colonies against Britain, providing first financial support and then military intervention.

In late 1781, American and French armies, supported by a French fleet, besieged the British Army at Yorktown, Virginia. Completely surrounded and cut off from reinforcements, the British General Cornwallis surrendered. Washington and his allies captured seven thousand British troops. These losses proved decisive; six months later the British Parliament voted to stop the war, and the American colonies had gained their independence.

The thirteen colonies had begun adopting new state constitutions in the late 1770s. These constitutions were among the most democratic ever seen. They broke sharply with European traditions by outlawing any distinctions of rank and title. Many had bills of rights to protect citizens from state authority and gave the vote to a wide range of male citizens (New Jersey even briefly gave women the vote but withdrew their suffrage in 1807). Relations among the states were regulated by the Articles of Confederation, which were ratified in 1781.

Yet the Articles almost immediately were seen to be inadequate. There were no rules to regulate trade or create a common currency among the states, and the central government was too weak to aid the states with their debts or manage national defense. So in 1787 a national convention met in Philadelphia to draft a new federal constitution.

Since most loyalists had fled to Canada, the new government faced no major internal counterrevolutionary threats, and once British forces withdrew, America was also secure from foreign invasion. Under these favorable conditions, the idea of a stronger central government was controversial. Debates dragged on and many compromises were made, including retention of slavery. But in a masterpiece of political argument, now known as the *Federalist Papers*, James Madison, John Jay, and Alexander Hamilton defended the new constitution. Harking back to the Roman revolution against its foreign kings, signing their papers "Publius," they successfully argued that America should become a representative republic, with a Senate, House of Representatives, and president, all directly or indirectly chosen by the vote of qualified citizens. The new constitution was ratified in 1788, and later that year George Washington was elected the first president of the United States of America.

3. After the American Revolution, disputes among the former colonies and concerns about credit and commerce led to demands for a stronger central government for the new nation. In 1787 the former colonies sent representatives to negotiate and draw up a new constitution for the United States. Howard Chandler Christy's painting of the signing of the Constitution hangs in the U.S. Capitol.

The French Revolution

The American Revolution seemed radical to Europeans, but it was also quite distant. Yet revolution would soon strike the largest country in Europe. Despite France's success in the American War of Independence, its accumulated war debts and the imminent expiration of wartime tax measures created a fiscal crisis. When French law courts and notables rejected proposed new taxes, the king was pressured to call a meeting of the representatives of the three estates of the realm—the clergy, nobility, and commoners—to seek a solution.

The Estates met in May 1789, after a year of famine had spurred riots across the country, and expectations ran high for major political and economic reforms. Yet the Estates immediately broke down into acrimony. The clergy and nobility insisted on voting by Estates, so that their votes would always outweigh those of the commoners, known as the Third Estate. However, the Third Estate was filled with professionals and bureaucrats who had sought or were even in the process of acquiring noble status themselves, as the eighteenth century had been a period of considerable social mobility; they were enraged at being treated as insignificant. Their rage was shared by abbots and priests who were also treated as commoners by the privileged bishops. The Abbé Sieyès wrote: "What is the Third Estate? Everything. What has it been until now in the public order? Nothing."

After weeks of deadlock, the representatives of the Third Estate proclaimed that they spoke for the entire nation. Reconstituting themselves as the National Assembly and joined by reformers from the other Estates, they set out to reshape France. They produced a Declaration of the Rights of Man and of the Citizen, and from 1789 to 1793 the Assembly, and the elected Legislative Assembly and National Convention that followed, abolished the monarchy and all feudal privileges, nationalized the church, and executed King Louis XVI and his elegant queen, Marie Antoinette. France was declared a republic, under the motto *Liberté, Égalité, Fraternité*. The French revolutionaries saw themselves as repeating the feats of the early Romans who had overthrown their king and founded a republic, depicting themselves in togas and calling their military leaders "consuls" after the old Roman term.

The actions of the national assemblies and conventions were spurred by popular uprisings in Paris and the provinces. In 1789, fearing that the king would disperse the new National Assembly, Parisian workers armed themselves and attacked a royal fortress, the Bastille. Supported by a detachment of renegade soldiers with artillery, the crowds took the Bastille on July 14.

Foreign powers grew alarmed and attacked the new republic. Within France, several provinces resisted the nationalization of the church and the new demands of the revolutionary government, producing a civil war as well. Under these strains, radicals formed a Committee of Public Safety. Maximilian Robespierre and his colleagues on the committee led a reign of terror, executing accused enemies of the revolution in Paris and the provinces by the thousands. Robespierre even had several fellow revolutionaries guillotined, but eventually he too was brought to meet Madame Guillotine, and in 1795 the radicals were deposed and replaced by a more moderate and pragmatic government.

French armies then spread across Europe, fomenting republican revolutions near and far. After 1799, the French Revolution came under the control of the wildly popular and successful general Napoleon Bonaparte. Napoleon advanced himself from consul to emperor, and like the ancient Romans, commissioned triumphal arches (the Arc de Triomphe) to mark his conquests. The Vendôme Column in Paris, modeled after Trajan's column in Rome, bears a statue of Napoleon wearing a toga and crowned with a laurel wreath.

4. A turning point in the French Revolution was the decision of an artillery detachment of the French army—prominently shown in the foreground of this painting—to support a group of citizens who sought to gain arms for the people of Paris by storming the Royal Fortress of the Bastille on July 14, 1789.

Napoleon's string of victories ended on the outskirts of Moscow, where he was turned back by the Russian winter and the stubborn resistance of Russian forces. After Napoleon was defeated by a coalition of European powers, he was exiled and in 1814 a Bourbon king, Louis XVIIII, was restored to the French throne.

Yet by then the belief that government belonged in the hands of citizens, not kings, had become widespread. The French Revolution—with its popular attacks on aristocrats, revolutionary terror, creation of a new constitutional order, and military success and expansion under Napoleon—soon became the prototype of a revolution for succeeding generations.

Even in France's sugar colony of Saint Domingue (Haiti), slaves and former slaves followed the proclamation that all men were equal and citizens, and rose up to demand their freedom from the plantation owners and from France. After years of struggle, led by Toussaint Louverture, a former slave turned prosperous plantation owner, Haiti became a sovereign nation in 1804.

The European revolutions of 1830 and 1848

In 1830 revolution broke out again in France, and also in Belgium and Switzerland. In France and Belgium, the revolutionaries created constitutional monarchies, modeled on Great Britain. In 1848 an even larger wave of constitutional revolutions swept Europe. These revolutions produced a republic in France, a constitutional monarchy in Denmark, a new federal constitution in Switzerland, and briefly drove absolute monarchs from power in Prussia, the states of southern and western Germany, Austria, Sicily, Lombardy, Hungary, and Romania.

These constitutional revolutions were led by professionals and students pursuing the ideals of the French and American Revolutions and pushed forward by peasant revolts and urban uprisings, the latter occurring in the wake of sustained population growth and spikes in food prices in 1847–48. Yet the elite constitutional leaders never made common cause with the popular groups. No broad cross-class coalition arose to overcome the aristocratic and military elites, who remained loyal to the monarchies. In 1849 Russian troops backed counterrevolutionary attacks by the armed forces of Austria and Prussia, which reversed most of the revolutionaries' gains outside of France and Denmark. The success of this counterrevolutionary thrust has led most historians to label the events of 1848 as a failed or abortive revolution. Even in France, the republic was short-lived. Louis Bonaparte, Napoleon's nephew, trading on his famous name, was elected as the first president of France in 1848. A few years later, like his more famous uncle, he staged a coup against the republic and named himself Emperor Napoleon III.

From 1849 to 1871 conservatism reigned in Europe, and it appeared that the clock was turning back toward monarchies. Yet this was not to be. In 1871, after Prussia defeated Napoleon III in the Franco-Prussian War, the residents of Paris proclaimed the city to be a revolutionary commune, freed from the erstwhile emperor. Although the revolutionaries were eventually suppressed by a national French Army, the army itself made no attempt to restore the empire. Instead, it proclaimed the Third French Republic; France has been a republic ever since.

The ideas of democracy and constitutional government continued to spread; the Italian states were united as a constitutional monarchy in 1861, and even the Prussian minister Bismarck began granting constitutional rights in Germany. In 1918, following Germany's defeat in World War I, a worker's revolution helped topple the last German monarch and install the Weimar Republic. By the end of World War I, every state in Europe had thrown off their absolute monarchies, and all but Russia had become parliamentary, constitutional regimes.

Meiji Japan

Constitutional government became widely sought-after outside of Europe as well. Identifying constitutional government with the military, technological, and economic success of the European powers, reformers around the world wanted to replace their empires and monarchies with constitutional regimes.

Japan had been ruled since the early seventeenth century by the Tokugawa Shoguns. These military rulers, based in the capital of Edo (Tokyo), were supported by aristocratic governors (daimyo) and a privileged class of warriors (samurai) who lorded over the common peasants and artisans. Yet in the nineteenth century, the Shoguns had been financially weakened by growing debts to the rice merchants of Osaka, while several of the daimyos had started to modernize their own military forces and administrations with

Western ideas and technology. In 1852, the U.S. Navy Commodore Matthew Perry sailed a fleet of modern steam-powered warships into Tokyo Bay in an impressive display of force. Sweeping aside all resistance, he imposed a humiliating treaty on the Shogun.

Having determined that the Shogun's regime was outmoded and incapable of defending Japan, modernizing leaders from two southern provinces undertook a revolutionary war to overthrow it. Proclaiming their loyalty to the Japanese emperor—who had been a ceremonial figurehead under the Shoguns—the leaders of this so-called Meiji Restoration claimed only to be restoring the primacy of the emperor. After they defeated the Shogun and took power in 1868, ending more than six centuries of Shogun rule, they revolutionized Japanese society and politics. The Meiji leaders abolished the rank and privileges of the samurai, created a legislative assembly (the Diet), and eventually produced a new constitution.

Rapidly adopting Western modes of education, military organization, and technology, yet retaining their own distinct Japanese national culture and unity, the Meiji regime presided over rapid industrialization and the development of a modern army and navy. In 1905 Japan defeated the once-feared Russian military, helping undermine the legitimacy of the Russian government and contributing to the soon-to-follow Russian Revolution.

The Meiji regime in turn became a direct source of constitutional change in China, as many of the leaders of the Chinese Republican Revolution of 1911 had studied in Japan. Sun Yat-sen, the leader of the revolution, organized the republican opposition from Tokyo.

Despite their uneven successes, the constitutional revolutions created a new template for revolution. Henceforth, "revolution" would not mean the mere overthrow of a tyrant but the destruction of traditional regimes and their replacement by new, constitutional governments based on universal rights and the consent of the governed. From its origins in America and France, this model has spread to become the dominant ideal of revolution today.

Yet for much of the twentieth century, this ideal was supplanted by another model: that of communist revolution.

Thomas Paine on the worthlessness of kings:

In England a king hath little more to do than to make war and give away places; which, in plain terms, is to impoverish the nation and set it together by the ears. A pretty business indeed for a man to be allowed eight hundred thousand sterling a year for, and worshipped into the bargain! Of more worth is one honest man to society, and in the sight of God, than all the crowned ruffians that ever lived.

—*Common Sense* (1776)

Thomas Jefferson on natural rights:

We hold these truths to be self-evident, that all men are created equal, that they are endowed by their Creator with certain unalienable Rights, that among these are Life, Liberty and the pursuit of Happiness.—That to secure these rights, Governments are instituted among Men, deriving their just powers from the consent of the governed,—That whenever any Form of Government becomes destructive of these ends, it is the Right of the People to alter or to abolish it, and to institute new Government, laying its foundation on such principles and organizing its powers in such form, as to them shall seem most likely to effect their Safety and Happiness.

—The Declaration of Independence (1776)

The Meiji Constitution of 1889 on the rights of Japanese subjects, creating a constitutional monarchy under the emperor of Japan:

Article 23. No Japanese subject shall be arrested, detained, tried or punished, unless according to law.

Article 24. No Japanese subject shall be deprived of his right of being tried by the judges determined by law.

Article 25. Except in the cases provided for in the law, the house of no Japanese subject shall be entered or searched without his consent.

Article 26. Except in the cases mentioned in the law, the secrecy of the letters of every Japanese subject shall remain inviolate.

Article 27. The right of property of every Japanese subject shall remain inviolate [and any] measures necessary to be taken for the public benefit shall be...provided for by law.

Article 28. Japanese subjects shall...enjoy freedom of religious belief.

Article 29. Japanese subjects shall, within the limits of law, enjoy the liberty of speech, writing, publication, public meetings and associations.

Chapter 7
Communist revolutions: Russia, China, and Cuba

Karl Marx and Friedrich Engels, the authors of *The Communist Manifesto*, observed that in early nineteenth-century Britain the conditions of industrial workers were appalling. Child labor, twelve- and even sixteen-hour workdays, and repetitive work in dark, noisy factories seemed to them inhuman. They concluded that although the revolutions of the eighteenth and early nineteenth centuries had overturned kings and brought constitutions, the benefits seemed to go entirely to the new capitalist class of bankers, merchants, and manufacturers. Marx developed a theory of history that argued for progress through a series of class revolutions: First the capitalists would throw out the absolute kings and hereditary nobles; then it was equally inevitable that the workers would rise up and throw out the capitalists. Marx predicted a global surge of workers' revolutions against the capitalists and the liberal constitutional states. They would be replaced with communist states in which all property was owned by society as a whole, not used to exploit the workers for the benefit of the capitalist elite.

Marx was only partially right. In Europe and North America, workers did band together but not for revolution. Rather, they formed unions and backed labor and workers' parties, which raised their wages, limited hours, and provided gradually increasing social benefits. Meanwhile, in the still developing and mainly agrarian states of Russia and China, intellectuals dreamed of making a grand leap from peasant societies all the way to communist states. It was therefore in these and other developing countries, not the advanced industrial nations, that communist revolutions occurred.

The Russian Revolution

In the nineteenth century Russia was the largest but most backward state in Europe. Its vast spaces and huge population were mainly composed of peasants in rural villages. Industrial centers were few, concentrated in the mining regions of the Ural Mountains and the factory districts of St. Petersburg and Moscow. Russia's ruler, the tsar, ruled absolutely through his aristocratic officials and massive military.

In 1905, following Russia's shocking defeat in a war with Japan, peasant rebellions broke out in the countryside, strikes spread through Moscow and St. Petersburg, and sailors mutinied in several ports. Although the disorders were put down by the army, the regime took fright and accelerated its efforts at political and economic reform. An advisory elected parliament (the Duma) was created and land reforms were begun. But radical thinkers wanted even greater changes. Vladimir Lenin developed the idea of a vanguard communist party, which would lead the workers and carry the peasantry with them, sweeping away the tsar and his nobles and creating a communist society.

The progress of reforms was interrupted by the outbreak of World War I. In the first two years of war, from 1914 to 1916, Germany inflicted huge losses on Russia. During this crucial period, even aristocrats were distressed that the weak-minded Tsar Nicholas II and Empress Alexandra were distracted by a wild Russian mystic and healer, Grigori Rasputin. Though Rasputin was eventually killed (a difficult task, for he was poisoned, shot, *and* drowned), his malign influence over the royal family undermined popular and elite respect for the tsar.

Russian elites demanded greater control over policy, while popular protests against the war grew. On International Women's Day, February 23, 1917, thousands of women demonstrated against bread shortages in the capital. The following week, hundreds of thousands of workers and students joined the protests. When soldiers fired on the crowds, other military units defected and joined the insurgents, who attacked police stations and tsarist officials. The Duma claimed that only the tsar's abdication would restore order, and it quickly moved to establish a provisional government. On March 2, Nicholas II abdicated, ending the reign of the Romanovs.

The provisional government, however, was determined to continue the war. This provoked the anger of the industrial workers of Moscow and St. Petersburg and of peasants throughout the country. Workers organized themselves into councils (called soviets) and were recruited by the communists. Soldiers and sailors began to defect. A few months later, in October 1917, Lenin's vanguard communist party, the Bolsheviks, was able to stage a bloodless coup, organizing its supporters to silently take over the post offices, railroads, and government buildings of the capital in the dead of night. On October 25th, Russia awoke to find itself with a new communist government.

But taking control of the entire country would not be so easy. Though the communists quickly made peace with Germany, former Tsarist generals raised a counterrevolutionary, anticommunist White Army to take back the country from the "reds." Lenin's communists, with the organizational genius of Leon Trotsky, created a Red Army from defecting soldiers, supportive workers, and drafted peasants. Civil war raged from 1918 to 1921, fought with ruthless brutality on both sides. To

5. The Bolshevik takeover of the Russian government in the Kremlin in November 1917, led by V. I. Lenin and Leon Trotsky, led to a violent war between conservative landowners and former military officers and the popular Bolshevik forces. It also produced the first wide use of propaganda posters in a revolutionary conflict. In this poster, used by conservatives to try to discredit the Bolsheviks, Leon Trotsky is depicted as a "red" monster perched atop the Kremlin walls, overlooking the victims of the Bolsheviks, executed at his order by Chinese accomplices.

prevent the tsar's family from becoming a rallying point, they were all executed, even the children. Compelling experienced officers to fight for them, and drawing on the greater support of workers and peasants for the communists, the Red Army triumphed.

During the civil war, Lenin enforced "war communism" in which the party took total control of the economy and claimed all assets. After the war, in order to speed recovery from the devastation, Lenin adopted a New Economic Policy (NEP) that allowed peasants and small businesses to sell their products in local markets. But after Lenin's death in 1924, a struggle for leadership arose between those who wanted to continue with the NEP and those who sought to restore full communist control of all sectors of the economy. The latter faction, led by Joseph Stalin, won this battle, and Stalin became the new leader of the Communist Party.

In the 1930s Stalin carried out a ruthless program of collectivization of peasant farms, draining food from the countryside to invest in a crash industrialization program. Millions of peasants perished as Stalin's forces scoured the countryside, seizing crops and livestock to raise money to build factories and feed urban workers. When faced with opposition to his policies, Stalin unleashed a terror campaign of purges, show trials, and executions of his enemies, creating a vast "gulag" of prisons all across the Soviet Union. Even Trotsky had to flee, only to be assassinated while overseas.

Stalin's efforts to create a modern industrial base helped the Soviet Union defeat Nazi Germany during World War II and become a global superpower after the war, when the Soviets created and supported communist regimes all across Eastern Europe. Nonetheless, the Soviet Union itself would fall to revolution before the end of the century.

China's Communist Revolution

In the mid-seventeenth century, Manchu invaders from the north had entered China and founded the Qing dynasty. Under Qing rule, China became the richest country in the world, admired even in Europe. Yet by the nineteenth century, Western progress in technology and arms had left China far behind. In the 1840s European powers and the United States began to take control of China's overseas trade, imposing highly unequal treaties. As the Chinese emperor's grip was weakened by foreign intervention, and strained by rapid population growth, disorders began to spread. In the 1850s the great Taiping Rebellion devastated southern China, killing millions. In 1900 an anti-foreigner movement known as the Boxers attacked Europeans living in Beijing. In retaliation, American and European forces occupied the capital and demanded huge indemnities from the Chinese government.

As its power waned, the Qing dynasty tried to reform and modernize China's armed forces, schools, and officials. At the same time, revolutionary organizations arose aiming to replace imperial rule with a constitutional government. These organizations drew support from officials, businessmen, professionals, students, workers, and overseas Chinese, all seeking to expel the Manchu rulers and strengthen China. From 1907 to 1911, in what is known as the 1911 or Xinhai Revolution, anti-Manchu uprisings broke out in many cities and provinces. In late 1911 units of the New Army—which had been created by recent Qing reforms—defected and joined the rebels to seize control of several major cities. The provisional government of the Republic of China was created in January 1912; the next month the Qing emperor abdicated, ending more than two thousand years of imperial rule. Sun Yat-sen, a physician and intellectual who had been an early anti-Manchu revolutionary leader, became its first president.

The new republic did not last long, for new power struggles soon emerged. In 1912 Yuan Shikai, an ambitious general under the late Qing, took over as president. Forcing Sun to flee to Japan, Yuan appointed generals to rule the provinces. In 1915 he unsuccessfully tried to restore imperial rule, with himself as emperor. When Yuan died in 1916, China dissolved and his generals became provincial warlords.

The following year Sun Yat-sen returned from Japan, determined to restore the republic. By 1921 he had established a military government in southern China, led by his Chinese Nationalist Party (in Chinese, the Guomindang, or GMD). When Sun died in 1925, Chiang Kai-shek, a general who had fought for Sun, became the new Nationalist Party leader.

Meanwhile, Mao Zedong, the son of a peasant grain merchant, had graduated from college in 1918 and moved to Beijing. There he joined a group of scholars who, following the communist revolution in Russia, were drawn to Marxism-Leninism. Mao became an early leader of the Chinese Communist Party (CCP), founded in 1921. Still, it would take almost three decades of organizing and civil war before Mao would come to power.

From 1922 to 1927, the CCP worked with the GMD, helping the latter to gain Soviet support. In 1926–27 the Communists and Nationalists cooperated in a major military offensive, known as the Northern Expedition, directed against the warlords. But in 1927 Chiang viciously turned on his erstwhile allies and began a "White Terror" campaign to wipe out the communists. Thousands were massacred in Shanghai that April, and in the following years hundreds of thousands of communists, communist sympathizers, and suspected communists were hunted down and killed across the country.

Mao then argued that the CCP should leave the cities and raise a peasant army to oppose the Nationalists. Forced to retreat far inland to evade Chiang's forces, in 1930 Mao established a rural base in Jiangxi in southern China. Carrying out land reforms and building up his peasant Red Army, Mao gained control of an area that he proclaimed the "Soviet Republic of China." The following year Japan invaded Manchuria, forcing the GMD to turn its attention to defending the north against the Japanese. Nonetheless, Chiang remained determined to wipe out Mao's forces.

In 1934 Chiang's Nationalist army surrounded Mao's base in Jiangxi. Breaking through the Nationalist lines, eighty thousand communists set out on what became known as the Long March to reach another base in distant Shaanxi in northern China. Fighting constantly and traversing more than six thousand miles of rugged terrain over the course of a full year, only about eight thousand arrived at their destination. But the trials of the Long March toughened the CCP leadership, who became legendary for their endurance.

Meanwhile, Japan was preparing to push deeper into China. In 1937 Japanese forces carried out a full invasion, taking Beijing, Shanghai, and Nanjing. In order to win more support, the communists turned to fight the Japanese. Building up their forces to several hundred thousand, from 1937 to 1945 they entered into a patriotic alliance with the GMD against Japan. Yet the differences between the GMD and CCP were becoming increasingly clear. The GMD remained based in the cities, and its leaders grew increasingly corrupt, benefiting from generous aid from the United States. The CCP built its base in peasant communities in the countryside; its leaders were known to be less corrupt, more efficient, and more concerned with the welfare of the population in the territories it controlled.

When the Americans defeated the Japanese in 1945, civil war resumed between the GMD and CCP. The CCP, with extensive help from the Soviet Union, built up a large conventional army. Meanwhile, the corruption of the Nationalists sapped the morale and effectiveness of their forces. The Nationalist government printed money with abandon, creating a galloping inflation; it also treated the populations of areas it liberated from the Japanese as traitors, imposing heavy requisitions and tolerating profiteering by regime cronies. Mao's forces swept the GMD out of more and more areas. Finally, in October 1949 Mao entered Beijing and proclaimed the People's Republic of China. Chiang and the remaining Nationalist forces fled to Taiwan.

Once in power the communists pursued revolution relentlessly. Following the Soviet model, they nationalized all farmland and organized the population into collectives. They also sought to build up an industrial base, following the Stalinist emphasis on heavy industry. Then in the Great Leap Forward of 1958–60 Mao broke with the Soviet Union to forge his own pathway to economic development. Where the Soviet Union had focused on creating an industrial factory workforce, constructing massive iron and steel works and new manufacturing centers, Mao placed his focus on the peasantry. Dreaming of a rural, peasant-led economic growth surge, Mao encouraged peasants to form communes, which would strive for vast increases in the output of iron, steel, and machinery through local "backyard furnaces." But Mao's dream soon became a nightmare. His strategy produced chaos, as poorly built machines fell apart and peasants melted down their farm tools to meet targets for producing iron. Neglecting the harvest and giving up their farm tools caused a catastrophic shortage in food production. While propaganda posters showed well-fed peasants bringing in bumper harvests, people were reduced to eating grass, tree bark, and insects; tens of millions starved to death. By 1960, Mao

乘風破浪各顯神通

6. The communist regime of revolutionary China adopted propaganda posters to depict its version of reality. This poster shows peasants celebrating a bountiful harvest (including hay bales and spools of cotton thread), borne forth on farm machinery with a military bicyclist and a Chinese missile (showing China's military power) in the background. Everyone looks energetic, well fed, and healthy. In reality, in the year of this poster (1958), China was suffering from widespread famine during the Great Leap Forward, when ruinous government policies led to a severe shortage of farm tools and crop failures.

turned over economic planning to his more pragmatic colleagues Zhou Enlai, Liu Shaoqi, and Deng Xiaoping.

Matters improved in the early 1960s, but by 1966 Mao became convinced that China was becoming too materialistic and had forgotten its revolutionary ideals. Mao therefore launched a campaign promoting "continuous revolution." His "Little Red Book" of revolutionary slogans, *Quotations from Chairman Mao*, was published by the army and became one of the most printed books in history, helping to create a personality cult around Mao and his ideas. In this "Great Proletarian Cultural Revolution," schools were closed and tens of millions of youth became Red

Guards, encouraged by Mao to attack CCP officials, intellectuals, factory managers, and professionals. Mao turned on his rivals in the CCP, driving them from power. Millions of university students and skilled professionals, including Deng Xiaoping, were exiled into rural villages to do manual labor.

After a few years, with schools and factories no longer functioning and armed conflict between rival factions threatening to plunge the country into civil war, the army stepped in to restore order. However, power struggles continued between the radical Gang of Four, led by Mao's wife, and more pragmatic party leaders. In 1976 both Zhou Enlai and Mao died, and the Gang of Four were arrested, ending the second radical phase of the revolution. By 1978 Deng had emerged as the new leader of the Communist Party.

The pragmatic Deng launched a campaign to completely restructure China's economy. A one-child family program was implemented to restrain China's population growth. Communes were broken up and land was leased to peasants, who were permitted to sell their surplus output. Towns and communes were encouraged to start enterprises and were permitted to buy and sell at market prices. Special enclaves were created to court foreign investment and produce goods for export, a practice so successful it spread to the entire country. The government made huge investments in infrastructure, housing, energy, and other construction, and encouraged stock sales and privatization of state-owned enterprises.

Today, China under the CCP has become the world's second largest economy, with vast modern cities connected by high-speed railways and poverty virtually eliminated from the countryside. China has also become a world leader in foreign trade and investment. Yet as China has grown richer the hold of the Communist Party has only grown stronger. The current leader, Xi Jinping, has removed virtually all rivals in a vigorous anticorruption campaign and has had his ideas added to China's constitution. The former European-run trading enclaves of Macao and Hong Kong have been fully absorbed into China, and the Buddhist Tibetan and Muslim Uighur regions in the south and west have been colonized and often brutally made over into Chinese provinces. A massive system of cybersurveillance limits online expression.

While Xi has become China's most dominating leader since Mao, China's future remains uncertain. Population growth has now reversed, leading to a decline in the workforce. Productivity growth has slowed as well, as the nonstop investment in housing, infrastructure, and factories has overbuilt and unbalanced the economy. The overbearing and erratic policy response to the COVID-19 pandemic, suddenly shifting from the most complete and oppressive lockdowns in the world to almost complete freedom with little preparation or precautions, spawned nationwide protests. As the economy slows and resentment against the coercive rule of the CCP spreads, one may wonder if there will be yet another phase of revolution in China's future.

The Cuban Revolution

Throughout the twentieth century, the growing economic and military power of Russia and China was enormously attractive to aspiring leaders in developing countries. Communism became the preferred ideology of many champions of the poor, as well as those seeking to free their countries from domination by Western countries, whether they were colonies of Western nations or ruled by dictators with close ties to the West.

In the 1950s, one of the dictators most closely tied to the West was Cuba's Fulgencio Batista. In 1952 Batista had canceled scheduled elections and used the army to take over the country, relying on the support of elites connected to foreign business investments.

Sugar constituted 80 percent of Cuba's exports, and almost half of sugar production was by U.S.-owned firms. American businesses also had extensive holdings in tourism, hotels, gambling, utilities, manufacturing, mining, and oil refining. Many Cubans saw the Batista regime as little more than a front for U.S. interests. While Cuba was more prosperous than most Latin American countries (its life expectancy was fifth highest), peasants and workers in sugar refineries and other industries resented the wealth and corruption of those linked to foreign interests and the Batista regime.

Fidel Castro, a brilliant young law graduate, had planned to run for Congress in the 1952 elections. But when these were cancelled, he began to hatch plans for an armed insurrection to unseat Batista. Castro's revolutionary campaign was remarkable for his miraculous escapes and good luck overcoming repeated failures.

On July 26, 1953, Fidel and his brother Raul, with just over one hundred followers, attacked the Moncada military barracks in Santiago, on the far eastern end of Cuba. The attack was a fiasco—almost half the rebels were killed and the rest captured. At their trial, Fidel gave a stirring speech against Batista, claiming that "history will absolve me." Nonetheless, the rebels were sentenced to fifteen years in prison. A year and a half later they were freed, as Batista sought to improve his public image by granting an amnesty to the Moncada rebels.

The Castro brothers fled to Mexico to plan their next step. There they met Che Guevara, an Argentine physician who had traveled around Latin America. Che had become a radical advocate for the poor and had been outraged by the American overthrow of a populist government in Guatemala. Joining the Castros, Che and seventy-nine other Cuban exiles sailed an old and overloaded yacht, the *Granma*, to Cuba, landing there on December 2, 1956. Shortly after docking, they fell into an ambush by Cuban military forces. Only the Castros, Che, and about a dozen of their supporters survived. This little band fled into the Sierra Maestre mountains in eastern Cuba. There they recruited peasants with promises of eventual land reform, schooling, and health care and trained them as guerrilla fighters.

That might have been the end, but the Castros, along with Espin, Sanchez, and other leaders, were skillful; using hit-and-run tactics they managed to evade and outfight the forces that Batista sent after them, and their ranks swelled. Meanwhile, urban revolts and strikes by other opponents of the regime were harshly repressed, leaving the Castros' forces as the only open resistance to the regime. As Castro's prestige and reputation grew, Batista became more aggressive; in 1957 and early 1958 his forces tortured and executed hundreds of middle-class youth and workers who had joined in actions against his regime. In March 1958, revolted by Batista's violence and seeing Castro as a moderate nationalist leader, U.S. President Dwight Eisenhower halted arms shipments to Batista.

After the arms embargo, morale in Batista's forces rapidly declined. In late 1958 Castro sent several hundred rebels toward the cities in the east. Batista's army refused to fight them, and Castro's forces took the cities of Santa Clara and Santiago unhindered. On January 1, 1959, Batista fled, and a few weeks later Castro entered Havana with enormous popular support.

After taking power, Castro nationalized foreign business operations and undertook land reforms. True to his word, he began national literacy and health campaigns, building thousands of new schools and clinics. Castro believed that only a communist-style revolution could bring justice to Cuba, given its long domination by foreign business interests. Yet for nearly two years Castro did not openly proclaim his intention to establish a communist state, fearing the United States would move to crush his revolution. After John F. Kennedy became president, furious Cuban business elites who had fled from the revolution convinced

7. In this rare photo of the men and women leaders of the Cuban Revolution before they came to power, they are seen as comrades in the plain uniforms of guerrilla fighters, during the period of rural struggles against the Cuban regime of President Batista (1956–58). From left, they are Vilma Espin, Fidel Castro, Raul Castro, and Celia Sanchez.

the American CIA to finance an invasion by Cuban refugees and exiles, which would overthrow Castro and restore democracy. The invasion took place at the Bay of Pigs on April 7, 1961. However, it was easily repelled as the Cuban population rallied to support Castro and the revolution.

Castro then proclaimed his intention to make Cuba a communist society and entered an alliance with the Soviet Union, even placing Soviet nuclear missiles in Cuba. This very nearly led to nuclear war between the United States and the Soviets, but after a tense standoff and naval blockade by the United States, the missiles were withdrawn. Nonetheless, the United States imposed a strict trade embargo on Cuba and restrictions on travel, many of which remain in place.

Although Castro remained a national hero for standing up to the United States, the economy did poorly under communism and survived only with support from the Soviet Union, and later from allies such as Venezuela. Castro encouraged thousands of his opponents to flee to the United States, where most settled in Florida. Those who remained in Cuba and dared to be critical of Castro's regime, even once-fellow revolutionaries, ended up in prison or executed. When Fidel grew too ill to rule in 2008, his brother Raul continued as the new leader of the Communist regime until 2021.

Castro's victory, and his defiance of the United States, inspired other would-be revolutionaries. In the years that followed, his old compatriot Che Guevara developed a new theory of revolutions in which he argued that a small band of guerrillas, a *foco* (focus) of opposition, could overthrow any unjust regime. But this was not true. Castro's band had benefitted from amazing good luck, from the brutality and corruption of Batista's regime, from the Cuban the people's deep resentment of foreign business and political interference, and the U.S. decision to stop arms shipments to Batista. Elsewhere, when aspiring revolutionaries tried to organize *foco* movements against more efficient military regimes, or against regimes that retained U.S. support, they were cut down. Che himself was captured and executed while working with a *foco* group in Bolivia in 1967.

Meanwhile, the Castro regime survived decade after decade, weathering the collapse of the Soviet Union and continuing to draw on Cuban nationalism and resentment of the U.S. embargo to shore up its support. But as in China, Cuba's communist leaders have discovered that it is impossible to grow an economy without some free market activity. The regime has recently encouraged international tourism and reformed the rules regarding small businesses, banking, real estate, and the markets for cars, computers, and consumer goods. It remains to be seen, however, how fast changes will occur under the Castros' successors.

Chapter 8
Revolutions against dictators: Mexico, Nicaragua, and Iran

The revolutions in Mexico, Nicaragua, and Iran have provided us with some of the most striking characters in the history of revolutions—the bandit leader Pancho Villa; the wily guerrilla leader-turned-president Daniel Ortega; and the forbidding Ayatollah Khomeini. Each led a revolution against modernizing dictatorships that had become corrupt, personalist regimes.

Personalist regimes often appear quite solid, as the leader has eliminated all rivals and taken all power into their own hands. Yet such regimes are also surprisingly brittle. Personalist regimes often alienate elites by concentrating wealth among a small circle of family and cronies. Much of the population may suffer from uneven economic growth, while those without prominent connections face blocked social mobility. Personalist leaders also often weaken the military by choosing officers for loyalty rather than competence. Isolated at the top, personalist leaders may rely heavily on foreign support and greatly overestimate their popular appeal. As a result, when an economic or political crisis arises, or their foreign support falters, they may suffer a sudden loss of elite support, face rapidly growing popular protests, and find they have an unreliable military. Personalist regimes, especially after decades in power, are often more vulnerable than they appear.

The Mexican Revolution

After winning its independence from Spain in 1821, Mexico experienced half a century of political tumult. Military leaders fought for power, with foreign powers often intervening, until in 1876 Gen. Porfirio Díaz took control of the country. Díaz led Mexico for thirty-four years, and although he tolerated no opposition, he brought a period of stability and economic growth. As president of Mexico, Díaz promoted foreign investments in mining, railroads, and export agriculture, all of which led to an expansion of the middle classes and huge gains in wealth for his supporters. At the same time, though, foreign interests increased their control of Mexican land and capital, while the incomes of peasants, workers, and ranch hands lagged far behind. Peasants saw their lands being swallowed by expanding commercial estates (haciendas). Many among the middle classes chafed at being politically excluded by the Díaz dictatorship.

In 1907–9 a sharp downturn in commodity prices afflicted the mining boomtowns and farms, and spread economic misery across the country. Francisco Madero, the son of a wealthy mining and banking family, started campaigning across Mexico for free and fair elections. Madero proclaimed that under Díaz, Mexicans lacked freedom and control of their own fate. As the 1910 presidential election approached, Madero presented himself as a candidate. However, Díaz arrested him and five thousand of his supporters; Díaz then was re-elected president.

Madero escaped across the border to Texas, where he declared the 1910 election invalid and called on Mexicans to rise up in revolution. A number of leaders followed his call. These included Emiliano Zapata, a charismatic village leader from Morelos, south of Mexico City, who had been fighting to preserve peasant lands against the encroachments of haciendas. Seeing Madero's campaign as a chance for land reform, Zapata raised a peasant army to fight against Díaz's forces in southern Mexico. Another who followed was Francisco (Pancho) Villa, a former bandit who joined the pro-Madero forces and later raised his own army from ranch hands and other workers in the north. Yet another was an ambitious senator from northern Mexico, Venustiano Carranza. Unable to defeat the fast-growing revolutionary forces, Díaz resigned, and in 1911 Madero entered Mexico City as a hero.

Madero was elected president with 90 percent of the vote later that year. But his triumph was short-lived. In 1912 local rebellions against his regime broke out, financed by former Díaz supporters. Madero also faced opposition from disgruntled popular rebels like Zapata who demanded more radical reforms. In the chaos, early in 1913 the commander of the Mexican Army, Victoriano Huerta, used his soldiers to seize power and had Madero killed. Huerta's actions triggered a new round of civil war. Carranza gathered military forces loyal to Madero to fight against Huerta and restore a constitutional democracy. He appointed Álvaro Obregón, a talented officer who had fought in the defense of Madero in 1912, as general for the northwest. Meanwhile, Zapata and Villa raised their popular armies to fight for land reform and worker's rights.

Following major victories by Villa and Obregón in 1914, Huerta fled Mexico. Carranza now entered Mexico City and took power. Yet the civil wars were far from over. Zapata did not trust Carranza; Zapata seized control of Morelos on his own and carried out land reforms to benefit the peasants. Zapata then forged an agreement with Villa to fight against Carranza and Obregón. Over the next two years, ferocious battles raged across Mexico. Obregón lost an arm and Villa's forces, who had struck across the border, were unsuccessfully pursued by an American force under General Pershing. By 1917 Zapata's and Villa's main forces had been defeated, although skirmishes continued. Zapata was finally trapped and assassinated in 1919. Villa agreed to retire peacefully in 1920 but was assassinated in 1923.

Carranza had gained political support by calling a convention in 1916 to draft a democratic constitution. Passed the following year, it permitted workers to form labor unions, prohibited child labor, required equal pay for men and women, and gave the government the right to redistribute land to the poor. Yet Carranza declined to enforce many of these provisions, moving cautiously on economic reforms and resisting radical change. Just before the 1920 elections, Carranza turned on Obregón, who had planned to run for president. This was a fatal mistake; Obregón was popular and turned his forces against Carranza. Now it was time for Carranza to flee. Filling a train with gold from the national treasury, materials from the archives, and thousands of supporters, he headed to Veracruz. But his train was intercepted by Obregón's forces and Carranza was killed. Obregón was then elected president in 1920.

In 1924 Obregón's interior minister, Plutarco Elías Calles, was elected president, running on a platform promising more land reform and workers' rights. But once in office, he instead focused on increasing restrictions on the Catholic Church, whose central role in Mexico had already been attacked in the Constitution of 1917. Calles saw the Church as a bastion of superstition and an obstacle to progress; but he underestimated Mexicans' attachment to their clergy and their Catholic faith. From 1926 to 1929 Mexico was rent by the "Cristero" war, with Catholic groups fighting government forces. In 1928 Obregón was again elected president, but before he could take office he was assassinated by a Catholic partisan. In 1929 Calles—then the minister of war but still dominating the government—made peace with the Church. Calles institutionalized his power by founding the National Revolutionary Party. This party—later renamed the Institutional Revolutionary Party, better known by its Spanish initials as the PRI—would go on to dominate Mexican politics for the next seventy-one years.

Carranza, Obregón, and Calles had all been moderate constitutionalists, less interested in land reform and workers' rights than in restoring economic growth. They had taken only limited action to satisfy peasants' and workers' demands, and had continued to allow foreign companies to exploit Mexican resources. In the late 1930s, after the global depression set back Mexico's economy, the revolution entered a second radical phase. Lázaro Cárdenas, elected president in 1934, had Calles and many of Calles's supporters arrested and exiled. Cárdenas believed the revolution had not gone far enough in helping ordinary Mexicans. During his presidency, Cárdenas undertook extensive land reforms, promoted new national labor unions and higher wages for workers, and nationalized the foreign-owned railways and oil industry. Cárdenas took control of Calles's party and solidified its hold on government by developing corporatist alliances with organizations representing peasants, workers, and professionals.

After Cárdenas's presidency, successive leaders ran Mexico as an authoritarian state, with politics dominated by the PRI and each president handpicking his successor. Only in 2000, after decades of economic growth had expanded the middle class and a series of economic crises in the 1980s and 1990s had undermined support for the PRI, did the party lose a presidential election and Mexico become a true constitutional democracy.

The Nicaraguan Revolution

In 1972 a massive earthquake struck the Nicaraguan capital of Managua. Although no one realized it at the time, the quake not only destroyed much of the city but also marked the beginning of the end for the Somoza dynasty, which had ruled Nicaragua since 1936.

Nicaraguan politics up to the 1920s had been a history of feuding families with private militias and repeated U.S. intervention. In 1926 a civil war erupted between leading families contending for the presidency, and the United States sent the Marines to help keep order. The United States trained and equipped a new Nicaraguan National Guard, which they hoped would defend the constitution after U.S. forces left. But the National Guard turned out to be loyal mainly to its commander, Gen. Anastasío Somoza, the American-educated son of a coffee plantation owner.

Augusto César Sandino, who led a guerrilla army in the war, said that the United States had chosen a puppet president to back foreign interests and vowed not to lay down his arms until all U.S. troops left Nicaragua. Sandino fought the Marines and the National Guard until 1932. Then, under pressure from the Great Depression, the United States agreed to remove its forces after holding new elections, and Sandino agreed to disarm.

But General Somoza did not accept the deal. In 1934 he assassinated Sandino, and two years later he deposed the elected president and seized power. Somoza ruled for twenty years, until he himself was assassinated. He was succeeded by his son Luis, who ruled from 1956 until he died in 1967. The presidency then passed to Luis's younger brother, Anastasio.

From 1960 to 1975 Nicaragua's economy grew strongly. In response to Cuba's communist revolution, the United States sent foreign aid to gain Nicaragua's support, and exports of coffee, cattle, timber, and rubber expanded. But due to rapid population growth (Nicaragua's population doubled from 1950 to 1970), restrictions on union organizing, and increasingly concentrated land-ownership, the benefits of Nicaragua's economic growth went overwhelmingly to the upper-class elites.

In 1961 a small group of Marxists—mostly educated middle-class youth inspired by the revolution in Cuba—formed an opposition movement they named after the Nicaraguan national hero Augusto César Sandino, calling themselves the Sandinista Front for National Liberation (FSLN). Yet they drew little popular support and were hunted down by the National Guard. Many were jailed and tortured by Somoza's troops.

The tide started to turn in the late 1960s. The Catholic Church in Latin America began to follow the tenets of Liberation Theology, which argued that the Church should help improve the lives of the poor and support struggles for human rights. In response several FSLN leaders, including the Ortega brothers, Daniel and Humberto, set aside Marxism and started to build a more diverse anti-Somoza movement that welcomed workers, peasants, businessmen, and clergy.

After the Managua earthquake in 1972, international aid poured in to rebuild the shattered city. Yet the populace and even business elites were shocked to see Somoza and several of his business associates treat this as an opportunity to grow rich. Somoza pocketed most of the reconstruction aid, investing it in his own land-development projects and leaving a third of the city in ruins. National Guard units seized and sold off reconstruction equipment and supplies. In the years following the earthquake, the economy slowed sharply, causing widespread distress to workers and peasants while Somoza and his cronies increased their wealth.

In the mid-1970s the Ortega brothers masterminded several daring strikes, kidnapping prominent Nicaraguans and ransoming them for funds, prisoner releases, and opportunities to spread their message via the media. Somoza responded by declaring martial law in 1975, sending the National Guard to spread terror in the countryside, and arresting and torturing hundreds of FSLN supporters. Pedro Joaquín Chamorro, editor of the newspaper *La Prensa*, began a campaign to expose the brutality and corruption of the Somoza regime, fanning middle- and upper-class opposition.

In 1977 the new U.S. president Jimmy Carter, who had promised to make defense of human rights a priority, threatened to stop military aid to Nicaragua unless Somoza dropped martial law. Somoza complied and released many of his political prisoners. This gave the FSLN a fresh chance to organize workers in the cities and build up its guerrilla forces in the countryside. Then in January 1978 Chamorro was assassinated, leading to an outpouring of strikes and demonstrations. Aid from other countries in Latin America started to flow to the FSLN.

In the autumn of 1978 Somoza reinstated martial law and ordered the National Guard to attack urban neighborhoods dominated by FSLN supporters with planes, tanks, and artillery, killing thousands. Business and religious leaders pleaded with President Carter to negotiate a peaceful departure for Somoza and broker a deal with the FSLN, but talks went nowhere. Even when the United States stopped all military assistance to his government, Somoza refused to leave.

In early 1979 crowds in many cities, including the capital, built barricades and took control of neighborhoods. Somoza ordered the guard to fight back, bombing Managua and shooting thousands, including an American television journalist. In May 1979 the FSLN launched a final offensive with coordinated urban uprisings and guerrilla advances into major cities. The United States and the Organization of American States asked Somoza to resign. The National Guard, now deprived of ammunition by the United States and demoralized by international support for the FSLN, started to disintegrate. Somoza left the country, and in July 1979 Sandinista fighters took control of Managua as the remnants of the National Guard fled to Honduras.

The FSLN first sought to rule with a broad coalition, setting up a provisional junta with business leaders and priests, including Chamorro's widow, Violeta, who had taken over *La Prensa*. In the first national elections in 1984, Daniel Ortega was chosen president, and the FSLN won a majority in the legislature. The FSLN immediately nationalized all of the Somoza family's assets.

But the alliance between the Marxist-leaning FSLN and the business and religious communities did not last. The FSLN threatened to nationalize more private lands and businesses. In addition, when Ronald Reagan was elected president of the United States in 1980, he saw the Sandinistas as no different from Cuba. He imposed an economic embargo and gave aid and military support to former National Guard members in Honduras to form a "Contra" army to harass the Sandinistas. As the costs of the Contra war rose, people began to look for an alternative. In the 1990 elections Violeta Chamorro ran against Ortega and was elected president. The FSLN also lost their majority in the legislature, although they retained nearly half the seats.

In the presidential elections of 1996 and 2001 Ortega ran again but lost to moderate candidates backed by the business community. The business leaders soon proved corrupt and did little to improve the lot of the average Nicaraguan. In 2006 Ortega ran again and won, and he was re-elected with an even larger majority in 2011.

Unfortunately, this was the last time Nicaraguans would have a free choice for president. Since his 2006 victory, Ortega has taken total control of Nicaragua's government, gradually weakening the independence of the legislature and judiciary. In 2014 the constitution was changed to allow Ortega to run for an unlimited number of terms as president; the courts also began to disqualify any significant opponents who challenged Ortega. All the major television stations passed into the hands of Ortega's family or close allies.

Ortega had thus himself become a dictator. This was clearly shown in 2018 when large-scale peaceful protests against his regime were met with a violent police response that left dozens dead, and hundreds were hunted down and killed by Ortega's police and paramilitaries. In 2021, despite widespread condemnations by human rights groups, Ortega was elected to another five-year term as president.

The Iranian Islamic Revolution

The last shah of Iran, Mohammad Reza Shah Pahlavi, claimed to follow in the line of ancient Persian kings. Yet in fact his family had come to power, like the Somozas, in a military coup. The shah's father, Reza Khan, was a general in the Iranian army who in 1921 led a coup against the Qajar monarchy and in 1925 took the title of shah (king) for himself, becoming Reza Shah.

Although Iran had a parliament (the Majles), Reza gave it little independence and ruled with near absolute power, enriching his family through exploitation of Iran's oil and acquiring extensive landholdings. Reza Shah also began a program of modernization, building railways, promoting education and public health, and banning the Islamic veil while promoting Western dress.

When World War II broke out, Reza Shah sought to remain neutral. But in 1941 Britain and Russia invaded and deposed him. In exchange for compliance with their demands for oil and military bases, the allies allowed his son, Mohammed Reza Pahlavi, to take the throne as the new shah.

After the war, in 1951 a popular nationalist, Mohammad Mossadegh, became prime minister. Under his leadership the Majles passed a bill to take control of Britain's Anglo-Iranian Oil Company, which produced most of Iran's oil. Mossadegh also demanded that more power be given to the Majles. The shah refused, and Mossadegh resigned, calling on the public to support him. Huge protests and strikes arose across the country; alarmed, the shah restored Mossadegh to office with expanded powers. However, Britain responded with an embargo on Iran's oil, hurting the economy and costing Mossadegh public support. In 1953 Britain and the United States had the CIA arrange a coup against Mossadegh that restored the shah to absolute power.

Had the shah then sought to broaden his base of support, he might have ruled in peace. But he became a personalist ruler, following his own vision and tolerating no dissent or restrictions on his power. He sought to limit the power and wealth of the clergy by breaking up their estates and distributing land to the peasantry. However, without estate owners providing fertilizers and maintaining irrigation works, peasants often were unable to produce enough to support their families. Millions of peasants moved to the cities, where they were drawn into the mosque networks run by the now resentful clergy and supported by the traditional merchants of the bazaars (*bazaaris*). Meanwhile, the shah joined with other oil-producing nations to drive up the world price of oil. Expecting a bonanza, the shah spent and borrowed wildly to acquire the latest weapons (supplied by the United States) and to modernize the economy. Yet his spending unleashed rampant inflation that undermined even the middle class and industrial workers. The shah chose to make scapegoats of the *bazaaris* for raising prices, imprisoning many and thus earning their fierce enmity. By the 1970s the shah had managed to turn virtually every sector of Iranian society—the clergy, the peasantry, the urban poor, the working classes, the *bazaaris*, and the professional middle class—against him.

The shah retained power by use of his secret police, which arrested and tortured opponents, and support from the United States. But in 1977 U.S. President Jimmy Carter, pursuing his policy of promoting democracy and human rights, warned the shah to allow peaceful protests and stop torture. This allowed strikes and public demonstrations to challenge the shah.

Many groups were involved in the opposition—communists who had influence with oil and industrial workers, liberal intellectuals and students who wanted to replace the shah's dictatorship with democracy, traditional merchants, clerics, and peasants who hated the shah's aggressive support for Western dress and culture, and nationalists who wanted to end U.S. influence. The most influential critic, however, was the Ayatollah Ruhollah Khomeini. Khomeini had been exiled for his criticism of the shah since 1964, staying in the Shi'a holy city of Najaf in Iraq until 1978, then in France. While in exile, Khomeini relentlessly criticized the shah for betraying Iran and Islam. He developed a plan for an Islamic Republic, which would embrace Islamic virtue, democracy, and Iranian nationalism. Khomeini's sermons and plans were smuggled into Iran on cassette tapes and spread throughout the country.

Following Carter's demands that the shah respect human rights, Khomeini encouraged large-scale peaceful protests. He believed the shah's soldiers would not attack peaceful protesters. At first, this proved wrong. When protests spread throughout the country in 1978, the shah's police responded with force, killing dozens. But Khomeini exploited the situation by proclaiming those who had been killed to be holy martyrs and calling for new protests to mourn for them. This created a cycle of ever larger protests, leading to "Black Friday" on September 8, 1978, when the shah declared martial law. On that day, according to Khomeini's claims (likely exaggerated), the shah's troops killed several thousand unarmed demonstrators. Workers responded with massive strikes that shut down the oil industry, devastating the economy. President Carter then told the shah he would not support the use of force. In January 1979, after weeks of massive street demonstrations, the shah departed for Egypt. In February Khomeini returned to Iran to great popular acclaim.

With Khomeini as the new leader of Iran, relations with the United States remained difficult. Fearing that the United States might act to restore the shah as it had in 1953, Khomeini continued denouncing the United States as the "Great Satan" and "enemy of

Islam." On November 4, 1979, thousands of Iranians stormed the U.S. Embassy, taking sixty-six Americans hostage. Since then, the United States has remained opposed to the Islamic regime.

In September 1980, fearing the spread of Iran's radical Islamic republican ideology and hoping to gain valuable oil fields near the border, Iraq invaded. The crisis prompted Khomeini and the clergy to tighten their grip on power. In 1981 Iran's liberal president Abolhassan Banisadr, who earlier had led the secular opposition to the shah, was removed from power and fled to France; by then, many of the leftist supporters of the revolution had been outlawed, with many killed while in prison. The presidency eventually went to another cleric, Ali Khamenei. Iran relied on human waves of attacks by teenage soldiers, stiffened by the newly formed Islamic Revolutionary Guard Corps, to repel the invasion. But hundreds of thousands became martyrs in a war that lasted until 1988.

In 1989 Ayatollah Khomeini died and was succeeded as Supreme Leader by Ali Khamenei. While Khamenei has remained in place since that date, the Iranian Republic has elected a series of presidents who alternated between relative pragmatists and more anti-Western hardliners.

The 2009 election pitted the incumbent hardliner, Mahmoud Ahmadinejad, against several moderate challengers. In a surprise result, Ahmadinejad was declared the winner. Following allegations that the vote totals had been rigged, millions participated in peaceful protests (the "Green Revolution"), challenging the outcome. However, Khamenei, the Revolutionary Guard, and the conservative clergy were resolute, and the guards and militia put down the protests. That has also been the case with further protests that arose over economic issues in 2018 and 2019. The Revolutionary Guard, which has acquired extensive business interests across the country, has remained fiercely loyal in supporting the Islamic regime.

At this writing, Iran is being wracked with the largest popular protests since 2009. They began in September 2022 with outrage over the death of Jina Amini, a young Kurdish woman who died in police custody after being arrested for not properly wearing her hijab (headscarf). Protests have continued for months and spread to include workers' strikes and protests over economic and political issues, with some protesters calling for the end of the Islamic regime. In response, the regime has imprisoned hundreds of protesters. Several have been hanged, others sentenced to death. Some have suggested that these protests will lead to yet another revolution in Iran. Yet at this writing it is too early to know where this confrontation will lead. What we do know is that revolutions often have aftershocks and further phases of conflict, and that the loyalty of the Revolutionary Guard will likely determine whether the Islamic regime survives.

Chapter 9
Color revolutions: the Philippines, Eastern Europe and the USSR, and Ukraine

Victims hanging from lamp posts, guerrilla warfare, terror, civil wars, international conflicts: These hallmarks of revolution lead us to view them as violent events. Yet violence is not the only way to overthrow a government. Disruptive nonviolent actions have also toppled regimes. These include marches and general strikes, occupation of public spaces, and refusals to obey government orders. Also vital are efforts to win over soldiers and actions to expose corruption and malfeasance. Such efforts can succeed if they deprive the government of resources, lead the military to defect, build a broad coalition of opponents, and cause foreign powers to abandon or pressure the government.

Nonviolent resistance works best where rulers depend on support from a democratic foreign power that will neither tolerate ruthless actions against a peaceful opposition nor pay a high price to back the existing regime. Gandhi's success in leading the Indian Independence movement against Britain relied on both the British public's repugnance at peaceful protesters being brutally treated and the high costs to Britain of Gandhi's followers boycotting British goods. The shah of Iran was similarly vulnerable when President Jimmy Carter of the United States (upon whom the shah depended for weapons and credit) insisted that the shah call off his secret police and permit the opposition to conduct peaceful demonstrations against his rule.

Where a loyal and determined military supports a financially strong and independent government, nonviolent resistance will usually fail, succumbing to harsh repression. Such was the fate of the attempted "Green Revolution" in Iran in 2009, the pro-democracy revolt in Burma in 1988, and the Tiananmen Square revolt in China in 1989.

Yet since the mid-1980s several factors have improved the prospects for nonviolent resistance to overturn regimes. First, global norms have moved strongly in the direction of requiring elections for regimes to claim legitimacy. Even dictatorships have felt the need to hold elections, though they often will manipulate the results to produce victories. When such manipulation is exposed, protests over flawed elections can become a powerful way to mobilize people for regime change. Second, new tools of mass media—including cell phones, YouTube, Facebook, Twitter, TikTok, and other social media, and international cable television—have made it easier for the opposition to acquire and disseminate evidence of regime abuses. Third, the rise of international networks of activists to provide training in nonviolent resistance methods has empowered opposition movements.

As a result, nonviolent revolutions have predominated in recent years. Sometimes called "urban" or "electoral" revolutions (when the mass protests stemmed from election campaigns), they are more commonly called "color revolutions" after the symbols adopted by the opposition in these events, such as the yellow ribbons worn in the Philippines and the orange ones in Ukraine. Other recent nonviolent revolutions include the anticommunist revolutions in the USSR and Eastern Europe, such as the "Velvet Revolution" in Czechoslovakia (1989); the "Bulldozer Revolution" in Serbia (2000); the "Rose Revolution" in Georgia (2003); the "Tulip Revolution" in Kyrgyzstan (2005); and the "Jasmine Revolution" in Tunisia (2011).

The Philippines' "People Power" Revolution

In 1965 Ferdinand Marcos, a brilliant lawyer, won the Philippine presidency. Once in power, he appointed his wife, Imelda, as governor of metropolitan Manila, gave high posts to his brother and sister, appointed his cousin head of National Intelligence, and handed out lucrative rights to timber, precious metals, and coconut plantations to his friends. The Marcos family grew immensely rich; Imelda was infamous for her collection of more than three thousand pairs of designer shoes.

Yet Marcos was also a shrewd ruler, bribing Congress to support him, controlling the media, and spending lavishly on roads, bridges, and stadiums to gain popular appeal. In a campaign marked by vote-buying, violence, and suspected fraud, he was re-elected president in 1969. In September 1972 Marcos declared martial law, justifying his actions by pointing to student riots and a growing communist insurgency in the countryside. He announced that elections would be suspended indefinitely, then ordered the arrest of his political opponents, including the popular senator Benigno "Ninoy" Aquino. Aquino spent eight years in prison before being granted medical leave to have surgery in the United States.

Marcos remained popular for the first few years of martial law, as he redistributed land from wealthy landowners to poor peasants and disarmed landowners' private armies (although mainly those of his opponents). But in the late 1970s, as the economy began to stagnate and poverty and unemployment increased, the Marcoses' lavish lifestyle became more repugnant and their popularity faded.

From 1975 on, Marcos relied more on the army, where politically loyal officers were given large raises and promotions ahead of more professional soldiers. Marcos also benefited from divisions among the elites, as the wealthy businessmen and landowners who resented Marcos's takeover of the economy and longed for a return to a democracy could never agree on a leader or common strategy to oppose him.

Then in 1983 Marcos took the lethal step that was his undoing. In August Ninoy Aquino returned to the Philippines. He was shot and killed the moment he stepped off the plane onto Philippine soil. Aquino's martyrdom produced two shifts fatal to Marcos—the unification of his opponents and rifts within the military.

Manila's Cardinal Jaime Sin encouraged the opposition to rally around Ninoy's widow, Corazon "Cory" Aquino. Cardinal Sin and several religious orders invited a pacifist organization, the International Fellowship of Reconciliation, to train union leaders, professionals, students, and clergy in the techniques of civil resistance. At the same time, the defense minister Juan Ponce Enrile and junior officers formed the Reform the Armed Forces Movement (RAM), which began meeting with the opposition. Corruption in the military also repelled Gen. Fidel Ramos, a West Point graduate who was passed over for promotion in favor of Fabian Ver, a favorite of Marcos who had masterminded Ninoy's killing.

After Ninoy's death, anxious businessmen began to move their money out of the country. Ninoy's funeral procession drew hundreds of thousands of mourners, and anti-Marcos protests and strikes went on for months. By late 1983 economic growth had fallen to just 1.1 percent, as against an average of 6.4 percent per year in the early 1970s. In October Marcos announced that the Philippines could not pay its debts and needed to reschedule them. The debt crisis triggered shortages of imported oil and food, and inflation leaped to 50 percent. Even Marcos's friends in the United States—whose largest air and naval bases in the Pacific were located just fifty miles from Manila—urged him to shore up his legitimacy.

Marcos called National Assembly elections in 1984. Printing millions of fresh pesos to use as bribes, dominating the national media, and ordering security forces to intimidate voters, Marcos again led his party to victory. Flush with success, Marcos scheduled a new presidential election for February 1986, certain that he could control the outcome.

But this time the opposition was better prepared. With support from Cardinal Sin, who encouraged priests and nuns to lead local chapters, the National Citizens Movement for Free Elections (NAMFREL) organized half a million volunteers to monitor polling places and guard ballot boxes throughout the country. Their polling made it clear that Corazon Aquino had won a resounding victory. Nonetheless, when the official vote count was released on February 15, Marcos was declared the winner. The final tally was condemned as false by the Bishops Conference of the Philippines, American election observers, and even several dozen Election Commission tabulators who had walked out after seeing their vote counts being drastically altered.

The next day, Cory Aquino addressed a rally of two million people in Manila and called for a civil disobedience campaign to oust Marcos. Meanwhile, Enrile and Ramos were planning a military coup. They set up their base in Camp Aguinaldo on February 22 with several hundred RAM soldiers. That night, Cardinal Sin broadcast an appeal on Catholic Radio asking Philippine citizens to aid the rebel soldiers. By the next morning, hundreds of thousands of Filipinos had surrounded the camp to offer their support.

Marcos sent a tank battalion to crush the revolt. But the soldiers found a well-organized, cheerful crowd, trained and disciplined to remain nonviolent. In the front line, nuns kneeled with rosaries in front of the tanks, while pregnant women, grandmothers, and children offered food and water to the soldiers. Despite orders to move forward and use their weapons, the soldiers refused to kill unarmed, peaceful civilians. Instead they began to join the crowd. Over the next few days, nearly 80 percent of the army defected.

Television workers refused to broadcast statements from Marcos. On February 25, realizing that his power was gone, Marcos took the advice of the U.S. administration to leave, and he boarded a plane for Hawaii. People power had won.

Anticommunist revolutions in Eastern Europe and the Soviet Union

After the Nazi defeat in World War II, the Soviet Army occupied all of Eastern Europe. The Soviet Union then supported local communist parties in taking over the governments of Bulgaria, Czechoslovakia, Hungary, Poland, and Romania. The Soviets also turned their occupied portion of Germany into the new communist-ruled state of East Germany, excepting only the western portion of Berlin, still occupied by the Allies. The changes were not always accepted; the Soviets had to send tanks to crush anticommunist rebellions in Hungary in 1956 and Czechoslovakia in 1968. They also had to build walls across Berlin and around East Germany to keep East Germans from fleeing west. Nonetheless, backed by their secret police and the Soviet Army and controlling the economy, the media, travel, and employment, the communist regimes kept their iron grip, tolerating no dissent.

At first, these regimes enjoyed some economic success, rebuilding from the devastation of World War II. Copying and adapting designs from the West, they built powerful heavy industrial economies. But the lack of any market incentives or individual freedoms eventually undermined their production. Ever-larger investments simply produced ever-larger piles of substandard steel, tractors that broke down and lay idle for want of spare parts, and stockpiles of oil, cement, and other goods produced to meet a plan rather than market demand. High-quality consumer goods remained scarce. Agriculture was a major failure, never achieving the productivity reached in Europe, the United States, or Japan. Keeping pace with American military spending and Western technological progress grew ever more costly and difficult.

With Stalin's death in 1953, communist leaders saw the need for reforms. They trained millions of engineers, technicians, and other professionals, while meeting consumer demand by increasing imports from the West. Yet by the late 1970s, this strategy produced enormous corruption, as party leaders controlled access to desired imported goods, while engineers and professionals were frustrated by Communist Party control of all enterprises. Spending on imports led to spiraling state debts, even as the centrally planned economy consumed huge amounts of investment while providing less and less growth. When Mikhail Gorbachev was elected the youngest ever general secretary of the Communist Party of the Soviet Union (CPSU) in 1985, he already had a plan for major changes.

Gorbachev aimed to root out corruption and advance a new generation of communist leaders. His chosen tools were twofold: glasnost—opening up information flows to expose the wrongs of corrupt CPSU leaders—and perestroika—restructuring government to introduce more democracy. Gorbachev believed that given a choice, people would choose leaders bent on efficiency, reform, and economic improvement.

Unfortunately for Gorbachev, by the late 1980s all of the communist economies were in serious decline. Discontent among workers over stagnant pay, elite corruption, and living conditions that lagged far behind the West was rampant. Intellectuals and workers throughout Eastern Europe's communist bloc demanded their own versions of glasnost and perestroika, and Gorbachev made it clear that the Soviet military was not available to intervene.

In Poland the Solidarity movement of workers, intellectuals, and clergy, led by the skilled shipyard workers of Gdansk, was driven underground by martial law in 1981 but revived in the mid-1980s. After major strikes in 1988, the Polish government agreed with Solidarity on terms to hold new elections, believing it could still win the majority of seats. In fact, Solidarity won every seat it contested, while Communist Party candidates could not even obtain the 50 percent of votes needed to win uncontested seats. In 1989 the new Solidarity-led parliament took control of the government. Lech Wałęsa, leader of the shipyard workers and co-founder of Solidarity, was elected president in 1990.

Throughout 1989 in Hungary and Czechoslovakia marches and demonstrations filled the streets and squares with hundreds of thousands of people calling for change. Deprived of Soviet support, deserted by intellectuals, and reluctant to use their military against peaceful protesters, the leaders of these countries agreed to hold elections that would turn the communist parties out of office. In Bulgaria a reform faction in the Communist Party itself took control and led a transition to democracy. And in Romania, ruled by the megalomaniac Nicolae Ceauçescu, crowds

8. In 1989 peaceful crowds of protesters filled the streets and squares of cities across Eastern Europe, demanding the resignation of communist governments. This photograph shows the extent of the crowds converging on Wenceslas Square in central Prague, which led to Czechoslovakia's "Velvet" Revolution.

in the capital and then the army turned on the dictator, who was captured and executed.

In East Germany, by October 1989 hundreds of thousands of the best and brightest had taken advantage of the changes in Eastern Europe to flee to West Germany via Hungary. After weeks of massive public demonstrations in Leipzig, East Berlin, and other cities, and told by Gorbachev that they could not count on Soviet support if they used armed force, the government gave in and allowed free movement to the West. On November 9, thousands of citizens swarmed the checkpoints and joyously tore down the Berlin Wall. In the following weeks Communist control disintegrated, and by 1990 East Germany itself had ceased to exist, having reunited with West Germany.

Yet the most dramatic changes occurred in the Soviet Union. In 1986 an explosion at the Chernobyl nuclear plant sprayed large parts of the Ukraine with radioactive fallout, gravely discrediting the CPSU. Instead of supporting reform-minded communist leaders, people began to back nationalist anticommunist politicians. From Azerbaijan to Estonia, millions of people took part in demonstrations demanding greater autonomy—and even secession—for the Soviet Union's national republics. In 1987 Boris Yeltsin, a popular reform leader in Russia, was removed from the Communist Party's ruling Politburo; in June 1991, running as a Russian nationalist candidate, he was elected president of the Russian Federation. Gorbachev grew uneasy with what his reforms had unleashed and tried to crack down on these movements. But by spring of 1991, after a wave of strikes throughout the country and demonstrations by hundreds of thousands of pro-democracy protesters in Moscow, he retreated and proposed a new constitution that would give far-reaching autonomy to the national republics.

This was too much for hardliners in the Communist Party, the military, and the secret police, who plotted a coup to remove

Gorbachev from office and reverse his reforms. In August 1991 the coup plotters held Gorbachev in his summer home in Crimea while they tried to take control of Moscow. They seized the Kremlin and major television stations, and sent tanks into the streets. Yet they failed to arrest Yeltsin, who called for his supporters to gather at the Russian Parliament building, where they began to build barricades and called on all Russians to defy the coup. On August 20 the coup leaders ordered paratroopers, three tank companies, and a helicopter squadron to attack the Parliament building. But key military officers refused and ordered their troops away from the building. The coup then quickly fell apart as the population and much of the military rallied to Yeltsin as president of the Russian Federation. When Gorbachev returned to Moscow, he found he had been effectively replaced by Yeltsin as the national leader. On August 24 he resigned as CPSU general secretary, and over the following months, the Soviet Union dissolved. One after another, from September through December, the former Soviet Socialist Republics voted to become independent states.

The Orange Revolution in Ukraine

The collapse of the Soviet Union did not produce the same outcomes everywhere. In Eastern Europe and the Baltic states (Estonia, Latvia, and Lithuania), most countries had prior experience with democracy before World War II. The new regimes in these countries, aided by the promise of future integration into the European Union, moved toward becoming liberal constitutional democracies. By 2013 all of these countries had been accepted into the EU.

Russia itself, however, fell back into authoritarian ways. The Communist Party was gone, but Yeltsin proved to be an erratic leader. Under his presidency, Russia was rocked by rebellions and economic crises. He was succeeded by a former KGB officer, Vladimir Putin, who promised to continue modernizing Russia while also strengthening the government. Exploiting Russia's vast oil and natural gas resources, Putin rebuilt cities, courted foreign investors, and increased state pensions and welfare support. He also encouraged a vigorous private sector, but drove out political opponents and gave the jewels of the economy—key firms in banking, railroads, media and publishing, and mining and natural resources—to friends in the security forces and to wealthy "oligarchs" in return for their political loyalty.

In other former Soviet Republics in Central Asia and the Caucasus, a similar pattern prevailed, with former communist strongmen emerging as presidents, using patronage and corruption to maintain power.

The people of Ukraine had hoped for a better outcome. In 1994 Leonid Kuchma, an engineer and early critic of the Communist Party, was elected president on a platform of economic reforms. During his second term in office, he was implicated in varied crimes and corruption, including the brutal murder of a journalist. Rather than seek a third term, he backed his prime minister, Viktor Yanukovych, for president in 2004. His main opponent was Viktor Yushchenko, a former prime minister who led a coalition of reformers including Yulia Tymoshenko.

The election was fiercely contested. Kuchma and Yanukovych used their control of the government and media to intimidate the opposition. Yushchenko was poisoned under mysterious circumstances; although badly disfigured, he survived and returned to the race. The first round of the election produced no clear winner, so a runoff was held on November 21. Exit polls showed a clear win for Yushchenko, but television reports showed Yanukovych with a surprising lead. Additional votes for Yanukovych suddenly materialized from various regions, pushing turnout to more than 90 percent of the voters in those regions and over 90 percent of those voters apparently opted for the regime's favorite. Allegations of fraud quickly spread, and supporters of Yushchenko began to protest.

On November 22 protesters poured into Maidan Square in Kyiv, Ukraine's capital. Wearing orange ribbons for the color of Yushchenko's campaign posters, they called for a fair count of the vote. Over the next few days, the crowds grew to nearly a million. Yushchenko declared himself the true president of Ukraine and called for a general strike. Local councils voted to refuse to recognize the false election results. The military and security forces started to fragment, many units declaring for Yushchenko. With the security forces so divided, Kuchma did not dare order them to put down the protests. Still, Yanukovych refused to concede. For the next ten days, despite subzero weather, hundreds of thousands of protesters continued to turn out in many of the major cities to protest what they considered a stolen election.

On December 3, the Supreme Court declared the runoff election invalid due to fraud and called for new elections. These were held on December 26 with more than twelve thousand election monitors, many from overseas, observing the polls. Yushchenko won by a clear margin of 52 percent to 44 percent. He was inaugurated as president in January 2005 and appointed Tymoshenko as his prime minister.

Nonviolent revolutions have generally led to more democratic regimes and have avoided the huge economic and human costs of ideologically driven revolutions. Yet color revolutions do not always have happy endings. New leaders often face a legacy of weak institutions, divided elites, and a restive population. Especially in countries with little prior history of democracy, developing the trust and institutional frameworks for good governance takes time.

In the Philippines Cory Aquino managed to preserve democracy against several attempted military coups. Yet she could not achieve desired land reforms, nor could she curb the influence and corruption of wealthy elites. Aquino was succeeded by Fidel Ramos, whose term started with an economic boom. By its end, however, he was mired in the Asian economic collapse of 1997–98 and accusations of corruption. Ramos was then succeeded by Joseph Estrada, who was impeached for corruption, and followed by Gloria Macapagal-Arroyo, who was arrested for criminal electoral fraud. To show how little has changed, in 2022 Ferdinand Marcos Jr.—the son of the overthrown dictator—was elected to be the president of the Philippines.

In Russia Vladimir Putin has been in power as president or prime minister continually since 1999. His most vigorous opponents have been assassinated or imprisoned, while critical journalists have been found murdered. Rampant corruption continues to weaken the economy and undermine the legitimacy of the government.

In Ukraine Yushchenko spent his presidency in fruitless power struggles with his former ally Yulia Tymoshenko, which undermined support for both of them. In the 2010 presidential election, in which Yanukovych, Yushchenko, and Tymoshenko all ran, Yanukovych emerged as the winner. Once in office, Yanukovych restricted press freedoms and put Tymoshenko in jail, prosecuting her for abuse of office and other crimes. It was almost as if the Orange Revolution had not occurred.

As these episodes show, making a revolution is one thing, and one that can occur with surprising speed. Creating a stable democracy is quite another, and may take years or even decades to accomplish. Most of the countries that have had "color" revolutions have not made a swift and certain transition to democracy. Instead, they have had to struggle with corrupt elites who retained their economic power, weak political parties, unreliable judicial systems, and factional struggles. In many of them, backsliding and authoritarian tendencies have emerged. Even color revolutions conform to the general pattern of revolutions, in which the fall of the old regime is only the start of a revolutionary process that may take several years or even decades to fully unfold.

A prime example is Ukraine, where a decade after the Orange Revolution, another largely peaceful revolution—the Maidan Revolution or "Revolution of Dignity"—occurred. In November 2013 President Yanukovych reneged on a promise to sign a political and trade association agreement with the European Union that had already been passed by Ukraine's parliament. Instead, he announced that Ukraine would accept a financial aid package from Russia. Angry protesters again filled Maidan Square in Kyiv, demanding that Yanukovych sign the agreement with Europe. When he refused, protesters called for his resignation. Clashes between police and protesters grew more intense in January and February. Unsure of the reliability of his army, Yanokovych fled from Kyiv, and Ukraine's parliament voted to remove him from office. Russia responded by seizing Crimea and backing a separatist rebellion in Ukraine's predominantly Russian-speaking eastern provinces. Yet Putin's hopes that these acts would keep Ukraine dependent on Russia were disappointed. Europe and the United States supported Ukraine's resistance to the Russian-supported eastern rebellion and helped negotiate a ceasefire. In 2019 Ukraine held its freest elections to date and chose a former lawyer and entertainer, Volodymyr Zelenskyy, as president. Unhappy with an increasingly democratic and pro-Western Ukraine on his doorstep, in 2022 Putin invaded Ukraine, sending troops to capture Kyiv. To the surprise of most observers, Zelenskyy proved a remarkably capable wartime leader, inspiring Ukrainians to fight and obtaining massive military and financial support from Europe and the United States. While at this writing the war continues, Ukraine has repulsed the major Russian attacks, and Ukrainians are fighting bravely to preserve their democracy and their country.

Chapter 10

The Arab Revolutions of 2011: Tunisia, Egypt, Libya, Syria, and Yemen

In February 2013 Zine El Abidine Ben Ali, president of Tunisia for twenty-four years, was in exile in Saudi Arabia, having been tried in absentia and sentenced to life in prison. Hosni Mubarak, president of Egypt for almost thirty years, was under arrest in a military hospital, awaiting retrial for the killing of protesters. Moammar Gaddafi, who ruled Libya for forty-two years, was dead, killed by the rebels who overthrew his regime. Bashar al-Assad, whose family led Syria for forty-three years, was under siege, having lost control of large portions of his country, with the major cities of Aleppo and Damascus under assault. And Ali Abdullah Saleh, Yemen's ruler for thirty-three years, had been forced out of office; the following year Yemen's capital was captured by tribal forces.

The sudden collapse of these regimes startled and inspired the world. Yet a decade later, peaceful change proved elusive: either a new dictatorship had arisen (Tunisia, Egypt), the old regime survived (Syria), or civil war is ongoing (Libya, Yemen).

Tunisia: from immolation to revolution

It is a myth that the Arab revolutions appeared out of nowhere, spontaneously erupting from a peaceful and tightly controlled region. All across the Arab world, similar discontents were building, and strikes and protests had occurred throughout the previous decade.

Arab societies have one of the highest population growth rates of any middle-income region. This produced a huge and ambitious youth bulge, while also reducing the land and water available to farmers. Egypt, Libya, Syria, and Tunisia had all followed the pattern laid down by the Arab socialist leader Gamel Abdel Nasser in the 1950s, aiming to win support by providing generous subsidies for education, food, fuel, and other necessities, and promising government jobs for college graduates. But rapid population growth, combined with the highest dependence on grain imports in the world, rendered these programs increasingly expensive and impractical. By the early 1990s governments started to slash subsidies. In 2008 food riots burst out in Tunisia and Egypt following a spike in food prices; another such spike was underway in 2010. Wages for much of the population lagged behind prices, and while the Arab economies grew by recruiting foreign capital they failed to create sufficient jobs: youth unemployment in the Arab nations was the highest in the world, at around 25 percent. In an exceptional twist, unemployment was highest among the best educated, who expected professional or government jobs but often waited years to find one.

Tunisia had made great strides in educating its youth, but outside of the capital of Tunis, especially in the south, poverty remained widespread and opportunities were few. Resentment increasingly focused on the personalist regime of Ben Ali, whose family was notorious for corruption. Under his rule, the gains from economic growth were channeled to an ever-smaller circle of cronies, while the broader business community bristled at his family's constant demands for payoffs.

As Ben Ali found it harder to rely on broad economic growth or subsidies to retain popular support, he relied more on police intimidation to stifle any opposition. Turned loose, the police became increasingly abusive of ordinary citizens. As one example, Mohammed Bouazizi, unable to find work, set up a cart to sell fruit in the small southern town of Sidi Bouzid. Claiming he lacked a permit, the police confiscated his cart and publicly humiliated him. In desperation, on December 17, 2010, he set himself on fire in front of the local police station in protest. Bouazizi's actions resonated among Tunisians who keenly felt the lack of opportunities and constant harassment under Ben Ali's rule.

When a crowd gathered the next day at the police station, the regime responded by firing into the crowd, killing several, and then sought to seal up the protests by blockading roads and censoring the media. But it was no longer simple to keep these events hidden. While the regime exercised strict censorship over national television, radio, newspapers, and most internet sites, it treated Facebook as simply a social outlet and left it alone. Because Tunisia had a relatively large middle class, the percentage of Facebook users among young people was the highest in North Africa. News of the events in Sidi Bouzid and the brutality of the police response spread rapidly online, soon reaching Al Jazeera, which broadcast it throughout the Arab world.

Riots spread quickly through Tunisia's southern towns. As the regime responded with further acts of repression, which were broadcast on Facebook and satellite television, anger was felt across the country. A remarkable array of organizations stepped forward to support protests against the regime. The Tunisian General Labor Union, which had been organizing smaller strikes for years among miners, teachers, and other workers, now organized national strikes in major cities. Thousands of internet activists adopted revolutionary personas on Facebook and Twitter; lawyers, journalists, and even rap musicians openly criticized the regime.

The international news media painted the struggle in Tunisia as pitting an internet-savvy but much abused population against a greedy and corrupt ruler. Under these conditions, neither France nor the United States, Ben Ali's traditional allies, would lift a finger to help him.

By early January, it was clear that Ben Ali's only hope of survival was to use the army to restore order. However, General Rachid Ammar told Ben Ali that the army was a professional force that would not shoot at Tunisian citizens. On January 14, 2011, less than a month after Bouazizi's desperate act, Ben Ali and his family fled to Saudi Arabia. An interim government took power and new elections were held in October for a democratic regime.

Egypt: the pharaoh falls

As satellite networks carried the Tunisian protests across the world, resentment against other aging dictators gave way to hope and plans for similar protests. Still, other Arab rulers felt certain that revolution would not spread to their countries. Egypt's foreign minister dismissed the idea as "nonsense." After all, Egypt had a vast police force and highly professional military. In addition, having been a key bulwark against Islamist movements and maintained peace with Israel, President Mubarak had always enjoyed strong American support. Moreover, Egypt's military was deeply invested in the regime. Every president since Nasser toppled Egypt's monarchy in 1952 had come from the ranks of its officers, and the military had huge investments in tourism, retailing, real estate, and other sectors of the Egyptian economy.

Yet, Egypt's regime proved vulnerable. President Mubarak had been in power so long (thirty years, an entire lifetime for young Egyptians), and seemed so determined to hand power to his son, Gamal, that people jokingly referred to him as the "last pharaoh." More importantly, Gamal was *not* a member of the military. Rather, he was at the center of a small group of billionaires who had built huge fortunes by exploiting government connections and foreign investment in oil, steel, and banking. Military leaders looked with anxiety on the young civilian heir apparent, skeptical that he would respect and maintain their key national role and their economic empire.

Protests in Egypt were not novel. In 2008 the April 6 youth movement had staged protests, but the Mubarak regime reacted harshly to any opposition, and youth activists were frequently jailed. One, Khaled Said, had been beaten to death by police in Alexandria in June 2010. Pictures of his horrifically beaten face circulated on Facebook, creating an online community "We Are All Khaled Said," which built a large network of anti-Mubarak sympathizers. But most Egyptians remained passive.

9. In the Arab Revolutions people turned against dictators who had been in power for many decades. The dictators were mocked as tyrants who represented the past. Here, protesters put up a poster depicting Egypt's President Hosni Mubarak as an ancient Egyptian pharaoh. The Arab text reads: "Put the Egyptian Pharaoh on trial."

On January 25, 2011, anti-Mubarak forces organized a protest on the national holiday of "Police Day." The regime was well prepared, with Tahrir Square and other central places tightly patrolled by security forces. What differed in the days following January 25 was not the initial protest but the willingness of vast numbers of ordinary Egyptians to join the vanguard of youth protesters.

Three factors contributed to this change. First, Egypt had held a parliamentary election in December 2010. In the previous election in 2005, candidates from the opposition religious group, the Muslim Brotherhood, running as independents (their party was officially banned) had won eighty-eight seats. This time, Mubarak was determined that the Brotherhood candidates would fail miserably, and he exerted every means—arrests, media campaigns, and attacks on their financial resources—to ensure that nearly every seat in Parliament was won by his party or his allies. Mubarak thus extinguished any hope of reform through elections, leaving only protest as a way to achieve change. Second, experts in nonviolent civil resistance from Serbia's Otpor! youth movement, veterans of the nonviolent revolution that drove Slobodan Milošević from power, had trained members of Egypt's April 6 youth movement. They taught the organizers of the January 25 protest the importance of maintaining disciplined nonviolence, and appealing to soldiers and police as friends and countrymen. Third, and most important, the example of Tunisia, where street protests had just driven Ben Ali from power, was a beacon to Egyptians. If Tunisians could do this, certainly they could too.

On January 25 people in Cairo began converging on Tahrir Square from all directions, the crowds quickly swelling to tens of thousands. An even larger crowd formed on the Corniche in Alexandria. For the next four days fierce fighting arose between police and the people for control of public spaces. The revolution did not remain wholly peaceful—police stations and prisons were burned, and protesters attacked police. But by January 28, the police were in retreat; the vast number of people and their determination to hold their ground was simply too great for the police to overcome. It would require the army's tanks and helicopters to clear the squares.

On the evening of January 28 the military was ordered into Tahrir Square. Yet they refused to fire on fellow Egyptians. Soldiers took up positions around the square but took no action against the protesters camped there. As the streets rang with cries that "The Army and the People are one hand," the Muslim Brotherhood now joined the opposition, committing its organization and manpower to the cause.

The refusal of the army to disperse the crowds created an open-ended crisis. Both the United States and the Egyptian military, who had been in constant talks, were seeking a peaceful transition. But President Mubarak refused to step down. The protesters set up tents and barricades, determined to occupy Tahrir until Mubarak was gone.

On February 10, amid expectations that he would resign, President Mubarak gave a long, rambling speech in which he again insisted he would stay in power until his term ended in September. The next day, massive strikes paralyzed the country from Alexandria to upper Egypt and from Cairo to Suez. Seeing order dissolving, the military removed Mubarak from office.

The Supreme Council of the Armed Forces took over the government, promising to return power to a civilian regime once new elections for Parliament and president were held. In June 2012, after a passionate election campaign involving dozens of parties and a run-off, Mohamed Morsi, the candidate of the Muslim Brotherhood, was elected as the first democratically chosen president in Egypt's history.

Libya: the death of a tyrant

Muammar Gaddafi, who took power in a military coup in 1969, was the ultimate personalist ruler. Having nationalized the oil industry, he had little use for formal government. Instead, he used his vast petro-fortune to create a family-led, patronage-run state according to his own bizarre philosophy of *Jamahiriyah*, in which Libya was to be a revolutionary state run by General People's Committees. In practice, Gaddafi made all state decisions and ruled by decree.

Gaddafi fancied himself an Arab socialist and nationalist; he provided subsidies for the poor and expanded secondary and university education. But as in other personalist states, he directed economic benefits mainly to his family and close supporters, leaving the majority of the population with stagnant wages and high unemployment.

In February 2011 Libyan youth called for peaceful pro-democracy protests. The largest took place in the eastern city of Benghazi, whose population historically had often been at odds with the western region and its capital, Tripoli. Gaddafi immediately sought to crush the protests. He gave orders to shoot protesters on sight, and hundreds were killed in the first week.

Why was armed force much more effective in Libya than in Tunisia or Egypt? In fact, Libya's professional army, just like those of Tunisia and Egypt, chose not to fire on their countrymen. Most defected to the rebels, melted away, or stayed in their barracks. But Libya was unlike Tunisia and Egypt in two respects. First, it was an oil power, giving Gaddafi huge revenues that he directly controlled. He used this wealth to create a private army of mercenaries from sub-Saharan Africa, twice as large as the regular army, who had no compunction about killing rebel Libyans. Second, Libya remained to a significant extent a tribal society, not a nation. Special "regime protection units" commanded by

Gaddafi's sons and recruited mainly from his own tribe were especially loyal, willing to fight to the end against Libyans from other regions.

In Benghazi, the professional military chose to stay in their barracks, and by February 20 the protesters were able to overcome the police and take charge of the city. But elsewhere in Libya, Gaddafi's tanks, artillery, and air power pounded cities into submission, starting in Tripoli and advancing quickly eastward toward Benghazi. Gaddafi and his son Saif threatened to kill everyone who had joined the rebellion in Benghazi, saying that "people who don't love me don't deserve to live." By early March, with thousands already dead, Gaddafi's forces were poised to inflict a massacre to recover Benghazi.

Thanks to satellite television and social media, the whole world was watching and sympathizing with the rebels. On March 18 the UN Security Council passed a resolution authorizing the use of force to stop the killing. NATO air strikes immediately began attacking Gaddafi's artillery and tanks on the ground, and sweeping his planes and helicopters from the sky.

Once NATO entered the war against Gaddafi—for it was now a full-blown civil war—the rebels gained legitimacy and began to mobilize more effectively. In late March they began a series of counterattacks under cover of NATO air power. In the next few months, the rebels retook the major oil centers on Libya's central coast, while Gaddafi was weakened by a steady stream of defections. In late July Berbers in the Western Mountains opened a second front, attacking toward Tripoli from the south while the Benghazi-led rebels attacked from the east. In August the double-pronged attack produced major advances, and Gaddafi's demoralized mercenary army rapidly dissolved, many fleeing across the border to Chad, Mali, and Niger. By October the opposition controlled the entire country. Gaddafi, found hiding in a drain pipe outside of Tripoli, was captured and killed.

Syria: descent into civil war

Like the other personalist Arab regimes, Syria featured a hated, corrupt ruling family, great inequality, and a large frustrated youth bulge. But its ruler, Bashar al-Assad, felt he was secure. He was backed by Russia, who had a naval base on Syria's coast. Assad believed his opposition to Israel gave him popularity, unlike the pro-Western regimes in Tunisia and Egypt. Also, Syria was still a tribal, sectarian society. Assad's family came from a small and cohesive religious minority, the Alawites—and Assad had packed the military with loyal Alawite officers.

Nonetheless, emboldened by the other Arab revolutions, and especially the intervention of NATO against Gaddafi in March, young Syrians began a campaign of nonviolent resistance. It began with demonstrations in the small southern town of Deraa. Had Assad shown restraint, perhaps the movement could have been contained. But as in Tunisia, the regime's indiscriminate and brutal response to initial protests, captured on YouTube and spread by overseas Syrians anxious to see regime change, quickly spread across the country on satellite television.

Syria's cities were swollen with peasants recently driven from their land by a persistent drought, who had received no help from the Assad regime and supported the opposition. At first, the commercial center of Aleppo and the capital, Damascus, were quiet. Troops were dispatched to the smaller cities where protests had developed to deal with those whom they were told were traitors and foreign jihadists. But upon finding they had been sent to kill ordinary Syrians, many refused to shoot. Some were executed by their commanders, but this only increased the number of those willing to defect.

By late 2011 the regime changed its strategy. Instead of sending troops on the ground to attack protesters, artillery and planes were used to bomb neighborhoods held by rebels, and then special forces, dominated by loyal Alawites, were sent to clear the area. Though effective, the regime did not have enough troops to carry out such operations in more than a few places at a time. The opposition became adept at melting away in response to such attacks and reconstituting itself in other regions, but it also became clear that peaceful protests would not be effective against Assad. The rebels too changed their strategy, seeking to capture weapons and creating military units led by defecting soldiers to carry out civil war.

Throughout 2012 resistance spread, reaching Aleppo and Damascus. But the regime's core military forces held fast and repelled each assault. The rebels waited for the world to intervene to help overturn the tyrant, as in Libya. They waited in vain. China and Russia blocked any UN resolutions to aid the opposition. The United States and Europe were wary of yet another engagement in the region. They worried that simply shipping weapons to the opposition would result in even more deaths and that the weapons would find their way into the hands of Islamist extremists. Meanwhile, Iran, determined to protect its supply route to its Hezbollah allies in Lebanon, intervened to support Assad, providing money, weapons, and military advisors.

By early 2013 the struggle in Syria had become a major civil war, with tens of thousands killed, sectarian conflicts inflamed, and jihadists moving into local power vacuums. Large parts of Aleppo and other cities were in ruins, and battles raged throughout the country. In 2015 Russia gave full military support to Assad, turning the tide and helping the regime retake most of the country.

Yemen: tribal and religious revolution

Yemen, sitting at the tip of the Arabian Peninsula, where its mountains catch monsoon rains off the Indian Ocean, has long been the most fertile and densely populated of the Arab countries, a land of "frankincense and myrrh." Yet it has always been difficult to rule. In the north, Houthi tribes following a local Shi'ite faith controlled the countryside, while the south coast was dominated by the cosmopolitan port of Aden. In the middle lies the capital city of Sanaa, one of the oldest inhabited cities in the world and a gem of Islamic architecture. Most provinces outside of the north are Sunni Islam and have been in chronic conflict with the Houthis.

For over thirty years, from 1978 to 2012, Yemen was led by Ali Abdullah Saleh, a former military officer who spent decades carefully building a web of alliances, playing off various Yemeni factions against others to ascend to power. Saleh also cultivated the support of the United States, supporting American efforts in the Middle East to attack Islamist extremist groups.

While Saleh, in his words, "danced on the heads of snakes" in keeping control of Yemen, the country remained poor. Population growth was dramatic, nearly quadrupling from 1970 to 2020, while water and other resources hardly grew. Yemen had some oil, but those revenues simply enriched Saleh and fueled his patronage machine.

In January and February 2011, following the fall of Ben Ali in Tunisia and Mubarak in Egypt, urban protests began and gradually escalated, calling for Saleh to resign. Yemenis hoped that a new regime would bring less corruption and improved economic conditions. Yet the prospect of Saleh's departure ignited tribal conflicts as the various Yemeni factions jockeyed for power. Gun battles broke out on the streets of Sanaa, and on June 3 a bomb attack seriously injured President Saleh. Saleh was persuaded to resign, and Vice President Abdrabbuh Mansur Hadi was elected president in 2012. Yet Saleh did not go quietly; over the next two years he sought to return to power with the help of the northern Houthis. In 2014 the Houthis swept down from the north and captured Sanaa, and then in 2015 continued south to assault Aden, where Hadi had fled.

The Houthi successes alarmed Saudi Arabia, whose king, devoted to an orthodox strain of Sunni Islam, could not abide a Shi'a-dominated Yemen on his doorstep. Saudi Arabia and the other Gulf states therefore entered the war, fighting to restore Hadi as president, and pushed the Houthis back from Aden. Former President Saleh responded by trying to join Hadi and the Saudi side; he was then killed by a Houthi sniper in 2017.

The Yemen Revolution not only overthrew the thirty-three-year rule of President Saleh, but also unleashed all the religious, tribal, and regional conflicts that have afflicted Yemen for most of its history. In addition, the United States under President Trump strongly supported Saudi Arabia's military intervention, selling them advanced weapons, in part because a variety of Islamist extremist groups had taken advantage of the chaos to expand their activities in support of one or another side in the complex conflict, and the United States hoped to see these groups diminished by a Saudi victory. Yet at this writing, the conflict remains stalled, with Saudi forces and their allies in control of the southern part of Yemen, while the Houthis and their allies remain in control of Sanaa and the north. Whether a negotiation can ultimately lead to peace remains to be seen.

A revolutionary wave

Tunisia, Egypt, Libya, Syria, and Yemen all fit a common profile of states that suffer revolutions: A corrupt personalist regime that alienates elites and loses the loyalty of the military, facing popular grievances fueled by fiscal and economic strains and demographic pressures. In all these cases a broad opposition coalition formed around a narrative of injustice featuring greedy ruling families abusing their beleaguered people: "You dress in the latest fashions," crowds in Cairo roared at Mubarak, "while we sleep twelve to a room!" In Tunisia and Egypt, the army refused to defend the regime, and the rulers were quickly pushed aside. In Libya and Syria, portions of the army stiffened by tribal and sectarian loyalty did defend the regime but had limited capacity. In Libya, foreign intervention by NATO allowed the rebels to defeat Gaddafi in a few months. But in Syria foreign intervention was on the side of the Assad regime, allowing it to keep fighting, while in Yemen Saudi intervention prevented a clear victory for Houthi rebels. The causal factors and processes of these revolutions are thus familiar, following the patterns observed in revolutions throughout history.

Yet after the dictators were overthrown, the road ahead has proven rocky. In Tunisia, efforts at power sharing among religious and secular factions initially succeeded, but eventually broke down amid economic decline, with President Kais Saied suspending Parliament in 2022 and paving the way to take absolute power.

In Libya, secular, tribal, and Islamist militias all continue to act independently, defying efforts to create a civilian-controlled national security force. Many towns have been riven by militia violence and political assassinations, including an attack on the U.S. diplomatic mission in Benghazi that killed a U.S. ambassador.

In Egypt, events have followed a typical revolutionary trajectory, from honeymoon to polarization, then counterrevolution. Following the joy and outburst of new political parties formed in the wake of Mubarak's departure, politics devolved into a struggle for power between the two best-organized groups remaining in Egyptian society—the army and the Muslim Brotherhood. Secular liberal groups, despite their early leadership role, lacked a grass-roots base of support or national organization and were increasingly marginalized. When the Brotherhood candidate Mohammed Morsi won Egypt's first-ever free election for President, he signaled that he intended to pack Parliament, the judiciary, and the constitutional drafting committee with Islamists and sought to drive the army out of political life. His actions provoked a popular backlash and retribution by the military. Drawing on growing fears that the Brotherhood intended to impose a fundamentalist Islamic regime, and with considerable popular support, the army deposed Morsi and passed emergency laws to reimpose military rule. Former general Abdel Fattah el-Sisi was then elected president in 2014 and has since suppressed all opposition, killing thousands of protesters to impose a regime more brutal than Mubarak's.

In sum, the outcomes of the Arab Revolutions of 2011 have unfolded as most revolutions do: with postrevolutionary power struggles, in some cases civil wars, a key role for foreign intervention, years of uncertainty before settled governments emerge, and a tendency to slide back into authoritarian rule.

Chapter 11
Recent and future revolutions

In recent years, revolutions and attempted revolutions have grown increasingly frequent. To name just a few, mass protests have driven out leaders in Burkina Faso (2014), Guatemala (2015), Armenia (2018), Sudan (2019), Bolivia (2019), Algeria (2019–21), and Mali (2020–21). Popular uprisings against governments perceived to be illegitimate or unjust have become a common feature of global politics.

However, two major changes have occurred in this century. First, there has been a marked shift in the dominant type of revolution. Ideological and social revolutions have become rare (although they still do occur, as in the case of the Islamic State, which ruled a large part of Iraq and Syria from 2014 to 2017). The great majority of revolutions are now nonviolent urban revolutions, seeking to create greater accountability in semidemocratic and autocratic regimes. This is partly because the world has grown older and more urban, and such societies are more likely to choose nonviolent protest over armed conflict, and partly because experience has shown that nonviolent movements are more likely to achieve success. In addition, many volunteer organizations now offer advice and encouragement for nonviolent campaigns.

Second, governments have become far better at resisting revolutions. In the 1990s two of every three nonviolent movements for regime change were successful; in 2010–19, only one in three succeeded. For violent uprisings, the success rate has fallen even farther, from roughly one in every four in the 1990s to less than one in ten in the most recent decade. This change too has multiple causes. Protesters may have been too optimistic, seeking to create revolutions in countries that were not really in unstable equilibrium. Protesters may also have been overly reliant on online mobilization of support, which does not yield the same commitment or pressures on governments as grass-roots organizing and physical protests. States too have learned from prior events; they are much better at surveillance, using social media to disrupt the opposition, and working to retain the loyalty of the military.

Yet these trends may suddenly change. One further lesson from history is that revolutions evolve, and do so in tandem with changes in the international order. In the coming decades, the countries of sub-Saharan Africa will play a larger role in international relations, as their populations grow and their resources become ever more vital to world trade. Along with exceptionally young and rapidly growing populations, many countries in this region also have either personalist regimes or weak, corrupt democratic governments. This combination makes sub-Saharan Africa a prime candidate for revolutions (and indeed the frequency of coups and revolutions in this region has been increasing). At the same time, both Russia and China, with rapidly aging populations and slowing economies, have become personalist regimes. As they assert themselves as major world powers, the strains may weaken their leaders and give rise to widespread protests (as have recently occurred in China over its COVID-19 policies), perhaps even leading to new forms of color revolutions, where competition in cyberspace and artificial intelligence bots and communications play new roles.

We may hope that a day will come when all countries in the world will have stable, inclusive, and just regimes that are accountable to their citizens. At that point, perhaps revolutions will fade into history with other heroic tales of wars and the creation of states and peoples. But we are a long way from that day. So we will continue to see people mobilizing to change their governments in pursuit of social justice and creating new political institutions.

If the trends of the past thirty years continue, they will increasingly do so by nonviolent resistance and avoid the terrors of radical revolutions that prize ideological purity over human life. We may then see the heroism of revolutions predominate, while the horrors will more often be avoided. If nonviolent movements can bring together people of different faiths, races, and regions, perhaps they will bring what revolutions have always promised: a better, freer, more equal future for all.

References

Chapter 1

"No, sire, it is a *revolution*!": Anthony Lejeune, ed., *The Concise Dictionary of Foreign Quotations* (Chicago: Fitzroy Dearborn, 2001), 98.

Chapter 2

"We of the older generations may not live to see the decisive battles": Vladimir I. Lenin, "Lecture on the 1905 Revolution," in *Lenin: Collected Works* (Moscow: Progress Publishers, 1964), 23:253.

Chapter 4

"The King has been taken away by poor men": Alan H. Gardiner, *The Admonitions of an Egyptian Sage from a Hieratic Papyrus in Leiden* (Leipzig: J. C. Hinrichs'sche Buchhandlung, 1909), 16, 35, 53, 58.

"Death thus raged in every shape": Thucydides, *The Peloponnesian War*, [431 BCE], trans. Richard Crawley (New York: Random House, 1982), 198.

Chapter 5

"That the people are, under God, the original of all just power": George Macaulay Trevelyan, *England Under the Stuarts* (London: Routledge, 2002), 276.

From the English Bill of Rights (1689): English Bill of Rights 1689, "An Act Declaring the Rights and Liberties of the Subject and Settling the Succession of the Crown," https://avalon.law.yale.edu/17th_century/england.asp.

Chapter 6

"England hath been known for hundreds of years": Oliver Cromwell, "At the Opening of Parliament Under the Protectorate," 1654, http://www.bartleby.com/268/3/11.html.

"Give me liberty or give me death!": Patrick Henry, "Give Me Liberty or Give Me Death," March 23, 1775, speech to the Virginia House of Burgesses, http://www.nationalcenter.org/GiveMeLiberty.html.

"deriving their just powers from the consent of the governed": Thomas Jefferson, "The Declaration of Independence," 1776, https://www.archives.gov/founding-docs/declaration-transcript.

"What Is the Third Estate?": Abbé Emmanuel Joseph Sieyès, "What Is the Third Estate?", originally published in Paris, France, in 1789, https://pages.uoregon.edu/dluebke/301ModernEurope/Sieyes3dEstate.pdf.

Thomas Paine on the worthlessness of kings: Thomas Paine, *Common Sense*, Philadelphia, February 14, 1776, "Of Monarchy and Hereditary Succession," https://www.ushistory.org/paine/commonsense/sense3.htm.

Thomas Jefferson on natural rights: Thomas Jefferson, "The Declaration of Independence," 1776, http://www.archives.gov/exhibits/charters/declaration_transcript.html.

The Meiji Constitution of 1889 on the rights of Japanese subjects: "The Constitution of the Empire of Japan (1989)," Hanover Historical Texts Project, http://history.hanover.edu/texts/1889con.html.

Chapter 7

"History will absolve me": Fidel Castro, "History Will Absolve Me," speech delivered in 1953, Castro Internet Archive, https://www.marxists.org/history/cuba/archive/castro/1953/10/16.htm.

Chapter 10

"Egypt's foreign minister dismissed the idea": Cited by Marc Lynch,
   The Arab Uprising (New York: Public Affairs: 2012), 81.
"People who don't love me don't deserve to live": ibid., 170.
"while we sleep twelve to a room!": Annia Ciezadlo, "Let Them Eat
   Bread," *Foreign Affairs.com*, March 23, 2011, https://www.
   foreignaffairs.com/articles/middle-east/2011-03-23/
   let-them-eat-bread.

Chapter 11

Data on changes in the success rate of revolutionary campaigns are
   from Erica Chenoweth, "The Future of Nonviolent Resistance,"
   Journal of Democracy 31, no. 3 (July 2020), 75.

Further reading

On the causes and character of revolutions

Beck, Colin, Mlada Bukovansky, Erica Chenoweth, George Lawson, Sharon Erickson Nepstad, and Daniel P. Ritter. *On Revolutions: Unruly Politics in the Contemporary World*. New York: Oxford University Press, 2022.

Beissinger, Mark. *The Revolutionary City: Urbanization and the Global Transformation of Rebellion*. Princeton, NJ: Princeton University Press, 2022.

Foran, John. *Taking Power: On the Origins of Third World Revolutions*. Cambridge: Cambridge University Press, 2005.

Goldstone, Jack A. *Revolution and Rebellion in the Early Modern World*. Berkeley: University of California Press, 1991.

Goldstone, Jack A., Leonid Grinin, and Andrey Korotayev. *Handbook of Revolutions in the 21st Century: The New Waves of Revolutions and the Causes and Effects of Disruptive Political Change*. Cham, Switzerland: Springer, 2022.

Goodwin, Jeff. *No Other Way Out: States and Revolutionary Movements, 1945–1991*. Cambridge: Cambridge University Press, 2001.

Katz, Mark N. *Revolutions and Revolutionary Waves*. New York: Palgrave Macmillan, 1999.

Lawson, George. *Anatomies of Revolution*. Cambridge: Cambridge University Press, 2019.

Levitsky, Steven, and Lucan Way. *Revolution and Dictatorship*. Princeton, NJ: Princeton University Press, 2022.

Nepstad, Sharon E. *Nonviolent Revolutions: Civil Resistance in the Late 20th Century*. New York: Oxford University Press, 2011.

Selbin, Eric. *Revolution, Rebellion, and Resistance*. London: Zed Books, 2010.

Skocpol, Theda. *States and Social Revolutions: A Comparative Analysis of France, Russia and China*. Cambridge: Cambridge University Press, 1979.

Stone, Bailey. *Rethinking Revolutionary Change in Europe: A Neostructuralist Approach*. Lanham, MD: Rowman & Littlefield, 2020.

Surveys of revolutions

DeFronzo, James. *Revolutionary Movements in World History: From 1750 to the Present*. 3 vols. Santa Barbara, CA: ABC CLIO, 2006.

Goldstone, Jack A., ed., *The Encyclopedia of Political Revolutions*. Washington, DC: CQ Press, 1998.

Revolutions in the ancient world

Ober, Josiah. *The Athenian Revolution*. Princeton, NJ: Princeton University Press, 1998.

Shaban, M. A. *The Abbasid Revolution*. Cambridge: Cambridge University Press, 1979.

Syme, Ronald. *The Roman Revolution*. Oxford: Oxford University Press, 2002.

Revolutions of the Renaissance and Reformation

Kishlansky, Mark. *A Monarchy Transformed: Britain 1603–1714*. London: Penguin, 1996.

Pincus, Steven. *1688: The First Modern Revolution*. New Haven, CT: Yale University Press, 2011.

Weinstein, Donald. *Savonarola: The Rise and Fall of a Renaissance Prophet*. New Haven, CT: Yale University Press, 2011.

Worden, Blair. *The English Civil Wars 1640–1660*. London: Orion, 2009.

Constitutional revolutions

Bailyn, Bernard. *The Ideological Origins of the American Revolution.* Cambridge, MA: Harvard University Press, 1992.

Doyle, William. *The Oxford History of the French Revolution.* Oxford: Oxford University Press, 2003.

Huber, Thomas. *The Revolutionary Origins of Modern Japan.* Stanford, CA: Stanford University Press, 1990.

Kaiser, Thomas, and Dale Van Kley, eds. *From Deficit to Deluge: The Origins of the French Revolution.* Stanford, CA: Stanford University Press, 2010.

Klooster, Wim. *Revolutions in the Atlantic World.* New York: New York University Press, 2009.

Popkin, Jeremy. *A New World Begins: The History of the French Revolution.* New York: Basic Books, 2019.

Sperber, Jonathan. *The European Revolutions, 1848–1851.* Cambridge: Cambridge University Press, 2005.

Wood, Gordon S. *The Creation of the American Republic 1776–1787.* Chapel Hill: University of North Carolina Press, 1998.

Communist revolutions

Fitzpatrick, Sheila. *The Russian Revolution.* 3rd ed. Oxford: Oxford University Press, 2008.

Pérez-Stable, Marifeli. *The Cuban Revolution: Origins, Course, and Legacy.* 3rd ed. New York: Oxford University Press, 2012.

Spence, Jonathan. *The Search for Modern China.* 3rd ed. New York: W. W. Norton, 2013.

Trotsky, Leon. *A History of the Russian Revolution.* Translated by Max Eastman. Chicago: Haymarket Books, 2008.

Revolutions against dictators

Booth, John. *The End and the Beginning: The Nicaraguan Revolution.* Boulder, CO: Westview, 1985.

Kurzman, Charles. *The Unthinkable Revolution in Iran.* Cambridge, MA: Harvard University Press, 2005.

Womack, John. *Zapata and the Mexican Revolution.* New York: Vintage Books, 1968.

Color revolutions

Ash, Timothy Garton. *The Magic Lantern: The Revolution of '89 Witnessed in Warsaw, Budapest, Berlin, and Prague.* New York: Vintage, 1993.

Aslund, Anders, and Michael McFaul, eds. *Revolution in Orange: The Origins of Ukraine's Democratic Breakthrough.* Washington, DC: Carnegie Endowment for International Peace, 2006.

Bunce, Valerie J., and Sharon L. Wolchik. *Defeating Authoritarian Leaders in Postcommunist Countries.* Cambridge: Cambridge University Press, 2011.

Kotkin, Stephen. *Armageddon Averted: The Soviet Collapse 1970–2000.* New York: Oxford University Press, 2008.

Thompson, Mark R. *The Anti-Marcos Struggle: Personalistic Rule and Democratic Transition in the Philippines.* New Haven, CT: Yale University Press, 2011.

The Arab revolutions of 2011

Cook, Steven A. *False Dawn: Protest Democracy and Violence in the New Middle East.* New York: Oxford University Press, 2017.

Lynch, Marc. *The New Arab Wars: Uprisings and Anarchy in the Middle East.* New York: Public Affairs, 2017.

Recent revolutions in Africa

Berridge, Willow, Alex de Waal, and Justin Lynch. *Sudan's Unfinished Democracy: The Promise and Betrayal of a People's Revolution.* New York: Oxford University Press, 2022.

Harsch, Enest. *Burkina Faso: A History of Power, Protest, and Revolution.* London, Zed Books, 2017.

Index

Index

Revolutions

FUNDAMENTALISM
A Very Short Introduction
Malise Ruthven

Malise Ruthven tackles the polemic and stereotypes surrounding
this complex phenomenon - one that eludes him today, a
conclusion impossible to ignore since the events in New York on
September 11 2001. But what does 'fundamentalism' really
mean? Since it was coined by American Protestant evangelicals
in the 1920s, the use of the term 'fundamentalist' has expanded to
include a diverse range of radical conservatives and ideological
purists, not all religious. Ruthven investigates fundamentalism's
historical, social, religious, political, and ideological roots, and
tackles the polemic and stereotypes surrounding this complex
phenomenon - one that eludes simple definition, yet urgently
needs to be understood.

'. . . powerful stuff . . . this book is perceptive and important.'

Observer

THE FRENCH REVOLUTION
A Very Short Introduction
William Doyle

Beginning with a discussion of familiar images of the French Revolution, garnered from Dickens, Baroness Orczy, and Tolstoy, this short introduction leads the reader to the realization that we are still living with the legacy of the French Revolution. It destroyed age-old cultural, institutional, and social structures in France and beyond. William Doyle shows how the *ancien régime* became *ancien* as well as examining cases in which achievement failed to match ambition, exploring its consequences in the arenas of public affairs and responsible government, and ending with thoughts on why the revolution has been so controversial.

> 'A brilliant combination of narrative and analysis, this masterly essay provides the best introduction to its subject in any language.'
>
> Tim Blanning, University of Cambridge

www.oup.com/vsi